Bill,

Truly hope you enjoy the read.

Good Hunting

Josh

COLD SOULS
A Guide to Good Hunting

Joshua W. Sargent

Whittler Woods Publishing
West Ossipee, New Hampshire

COLD SOULS
A Guide to Good Hunting
by Joshua W. Sargent

Published by: Whittler Woods Publishing
                    P.O. Box 105
                    West Ossipee, NH 03890
Telephone: 603-447-4921
Web site: www.coldsoulshuntingguide.com
E-mail: whittlerwoods@roadrunner.com

Library of Congress Control Number: 2009908216

ISBN: 978-0-9824849-0-6

Printed in the United States of America

0 9 8 7 6 5 4 3 2 1

Disclaimer:
You should use extreme caution and positively identify any and all wild plants and mushrooms before they are eaten. Some will make you sick, and though it is very rare, we've all heard of people that have died from eating the wrong mushroom. This book is not an identification guide but is intended to spur you to further investigation, and get you started in the right direction. Several field guides that specialize in identification as well as someone who is knowledgeable about the plant or mushroom in question should be consulted before anything is eaten. In short, the author is not responsible for any harm that may come to you as a result of the advice contained within this book.

Cover and Page Design by One-On-One Book Production, West Hills, CA.

Dedication

To my wife Alyssa — Thank you for putting up with a hunting maniac, and keeping me around despite many nights spent away from home during hunting season, and other stuff that would land most men in divorce court. You've always encouraged me to chase my hunting dreams, no matter where or how far away they took me. And also to my daughter Isabella, the most precious angel.

Thank You to:

First and greatest thanks goes to God. Without Him, I am nothing, and He is ultimately responsible for any successes that I've had in my life. I'd also like to thank my dad *David Sargent* for always making the time to take me hunting and fishing when I was growing up. I've shaped my life around these pursuits. Thank you to my mother *Laurie* for giving me a chance before I had proven myself, and when no one else would. Thanks also to *Hal Blood* who had a greater influence on me than he realizes. Thanks to *Nathan and Kim Zipf*, who have been good friends, and who are an inspiration to the benefits of clean living. Thank you to *Richard and Amanda Hume* from Jack Hume Adventures for providing unbelievable adventures that helped inspire the writing of this book. Thanks to *Alan Gadney* and *Carolyn Porter* (onebookpro@aol.com) for guiding me through the book production process and helping to make this book dream a reality.

In loving memory

Uncle Lewis Fernald, a great hunter, and woodsman
Charles Mattocks
Dennis Wedge, a master woodcrafter
All of these men had an influence on my life in one way or another

Table Of Contents

Foreword

One of New Hampshire's greatest geographical features was *The Old Man in the Mountain*. It was a series of jagged rocky outcroppings high up on a mountain that when viewed from the side as a profile looked like an old man hence the name. In recent years there was a rock slide, and unfortunately it no longer exists. At the base of this mountain was a sign that read, "Men hang out their signs indicative of their respective trades: shoemakers hang out a gigantic shoe: jewelers a monster watch: and a dentist hangs out a gold tooth: but up in the mountains of New Hampshire, God Almighty has hung out a sign to show that there he makes men." (Daniel Webster).

Joshua Sargent is one of those men that God has made, molded, and carved in the mountains of New Hampshire. Part of that molding was making Josh into an accomplished sportsman. Josh has run successful trap lines for years where he has trapped coyotes, fox, beavers, mink, otters, raccoons, and fisher. As a hunter, Josh has been successful in taking white tail deer, black bears, moose, and caribou. These animals have been taken with his black powder musket, "Cold Souls" rifle, and his self-made recurve bow.

In recent years, Josh has shared his outdoor experiences and skills in stories that have been published in *Fur, Fish, Game* magazine as well as several other local publications. Now within this fascinating book is an exciting collection of short stories of Josh's hunts. This book is neither the typical how-to book nor does it contain stories of high-end guided hunts of fenced animals, but it is a book from the perspective of an honest New England sportsman that learned success through trial and error from a young age and continues to learn in his present day hunting. The tales are gripping, funny, and honest with admissions of both failure and success. Within the tales, Josh shares what has made him a successful hunter. He has also compiled intricate pieces of advice from other New England hunters in an attempt to help make other men successful in their hunts.

(You're in for a good read from a New Hampshire native. Read on and enjoy these truehearted hunting experiences, you will likely gain some knowledge that may make your next hunt even more successful, or rewarding.)

When Josh is not working, hunting, or wetting a line, you can find Josh enjoying time with his family. Joshua resides in Middleton, New Hampshire with his lovely wife, Alyssa, and daughter, Isabella. Alyssa was quickly introduced to Josh's passion for hunting. Alyssa, though knowingly, made the mistake of being married just prior to hunting season. After a short honeymoon he was off to Maryland for a week to go hunting.

Josh's trade is an artist of wood. He is an accomplished woodcarver with his chainsaw, hand tools, and lathe. He owns and runs his own carving shop on route 16 in Albany, New Hampshire, where he goes by the name North Country Whittler. If you are ever in the White Mountains, make sure to stop by the shop. It is quickly identifiable — just look for the carving of an American Indian figure that towers forty feet over his shop. Many wooden animal images can be seen within his shop along with one-of-a-kind wooden furniture. Bears are his specialty, and he has demonstrated that he has taken chainsaw art to another level; American Indian busts are intricately detailed with his hand tools; and his beautiful Brownfield Bog burl bowls are crafted with his lathe. He has a sawmill, and cuts wide, customs live edge, thick pine bar tops and counter tops. Custom or commissioned carved pieces are also considered.

Nathan Zipf

INTRODUCTION: THE HUNTS

If you want to read about hunts that all end with the taking of a huge "trophy animal" these stories are not for you. Some of the animals taken might fit that category, but mostly these are "down home deer hunt" type of stories. Taking a doe with my recurve bow was almost as exciting for me as taking my nicest buck. In any case, each and every successful hunt is cherished, and considered a trophy to me. The meat provided is just as important to me as the horns, something that unfortunately seems to be rarely mentioned when the subject of hunting is discussed.

Many years my time, and main focus is devoted to my business as opposed to strictly pursuing a big racked animal, and oftentimes, I will take the first legal animal I see. I'm not trying to diminish the efforts of the people who consistently take trophy racked animals in northern Maine, New Hampshire and Vermont each year. The amount of skill, and effort put forth by these hunters to be successful is on the same level that I have put into my woodcarving pursuits. They make the difficult look easy, and luck has nothing to do with them being lucky each year. I know many diligent hunters who take deer almost every year and have lived out their lives without ever killing a decent buck in my region. I'd say that one or two nice bucks over the course of a lifetime for the diligent hunter would be average. My life's experiences have led me to believe that northern New England is the hardest place to hunt whitetail deer, and any hunter taking a deer consistently from year to year in northern New England is a talented hunter indeed. The ones killing the big bucks in this area every year are the true super heroes of hunting.

Once, I had a couple of discouraged looking out-of-state hunters enter my woodcarving shop. I won't say what state they were from, but it was one where the deer population is immense. In their home state they were used to seeing multiple deer from their tree stands each day. They were leaving a couple of days early because in almost a week's worth of hunting neither of them had laid eyes on a single deer. I tried to lift their spirits by telling them that it only takes a single minute for an unsuccessful hunt to become a successful one, and that they should finish out their hunt. Despite my words of encouragement they were still bent on going home. Before they left one of them remarked that you would have to be a "true hunter" to find a deer in all those woods.

A final word on trophy hunting. The "trophy hunters" you see on TV Sunday mornings are propped up by gun manufacturers, and other companies trying to sell products. Thousands of dollars have been spent for them to sit in the "lucky seat," and pull the trigger. Far too often the "lucky seat" is contained within a fenced border. These hunters have nothing on the successful Yankee hunter hunting public land wilderness animals. I'd be willing to bet if these

Sunday morning "trophy hunters" were turned loose in our northern New England hunting grounds, they would soon become discouraged, and leave, as they possess little in the way of hunting skills or woodsman ship.

> *"Come forth into the light of things let nature be your teacher"*
> *~ William Wordsworth*

1

SEVEN IS A LUCKY NUMBER

As a young man, around the age of 18, I was out of high school, and there seemed to be a lot of uncertainties about my future. I was feeling some of the anxiety that most young people do when it's time to leave home and pursue a future in the big scary world of adult problems. And was therefore, greatly looking forward to hunting season that fall.

During pre-season scouting that year, I found a pinch point that seemed to have a fair amount of deer sign. A pinch point, for those of you who do not know, is a feature in the terrain that concentrates deer movement into a smaller, more predictable area. It could be a strip of woods between a field, and a body of water that the deer are forced to travel through.

The pinch point I'm referring to in this story was a strip of woods located between two beaver bogs. You may also hear me refer to a pinch point as a funnel, or a bottle neck. The opening of the muzzleloader season found me spending a fair amount of time at the pinch point. I found a nice big old hemlock tree in just the right location to watch the better part of the funnel. The 28-inch-diameter tree trunk made for a nice back rest. I cleared away the leaves at the base of the tree in case a shooting opportunity presented itself, then, I'd be able to noiselessly shift my weight if need be. The lower branches extended a good ways out from the trunk of the tree, and swept down toward the ground almost touching in some places. After a little bit of trimming to open up some shooting avenues, and at the same time being careful not to trim too much so as to expose myself, I had a nice natural blind.

The first couple of hunts did not produce any sightings of deer, but I remained persistent as I figured it would be just a matter of time considering the fresh deer sign. I had a nice narrow little ravine that I had been using to approach the area. The ravine kept me concealed, and it also helped to keep the noise of my approach from being broadcasted any great distance, and best of all it dumped me right out at my hemlock tree. The approach seemed to be foolproof, but on my third time hunting the area, which happened to be an afternoon hunt, I jumped some deer out directly around the hemlock tree as I approached. I quickly slipped into my seat, and noticed that the deer didn't seem to be terribly spooked. They didn't go far, but had just bounded out of sight off to my right as I could still see bits, and pieces and little glimpses through the whips. (Whips are small beech trees or other whip-like young hardwoods that often grow in very thick dense clusters, and can be tough to move through.) After a while I was convinced that the deer had moved off when I heard what sounded like a sheep bleating off to my left.

Being a young hunter, I had never heard a deer vocalize in the woods, but soon one materialized. I didn't realize it at the time, but looking back, I know that I had separated this deer from the others when I jumped them, and by blatting it was trying to locate the other deer. At this point as a hunter, I had only killed a couple of deer, so every opportunity was to be cherished, and truthfully still is, but a missed opportunity had a whole different level of devastation back then. I took aim at the doe with my open sighted .54 caliber muzzleloader and promptly missed. I've noticed that a lot of hunters will make up every excuse under the sun as to why they missed, and I even know a few who would have sworn that this doe was running flat out, and that's why they missed. The truth is I just missed.

As the smoke cleared the deer was still standing there in the little wet spot where it had been before I shot. Now I was trying to scramble to reload my muzzleloader with as little movement as possible so as not to be detected by the deer. In the meanwhile, the doe nonchalantly walked right in front of me, and finally with a nose full became spooked, and bounded off in the direction of the others, but only after approaching to within ten yards of me. If only I'd waited I would have had a point blank shot. I try to learn from my mistakes, and I think the lesson to be learned from this failure was patience. If I had been patient enough, and watched the deer's body language, I could have easily waited for an easy shot.

To say I felt pretty low about the missed opportunity would be an understatement. I didn't realize it at the time, but it was actually a blessing. The good Lord had better things in store for me this hunting season.

I gave the funnel a few days to cool off, and hunted some other locations. I was not having any luck seeing deer, so I was still being hard on myself about the miss. When I hunted the funnel again, the deer sign was no longer fresh which told me the deer had stopped using the area. The close encounters, shooting, and the scent I had left in the area had no doubt taken their toll. I finished out the muzzleloader season without hunting the area again, and also without seeing another deer. I had spent a fair bit of time hunting during the musket season, and now had to get back to focusing on work. I was given a fair, and square shot which is all any hunter can ask for.

Being the hunting fanatic that I am, I just couldn't shake the urge to be in the woods, so even though I had to work on the opening day of the rifle season, I stashed my rifle in my truck in hopes that I might be able to get out early, and hit the funnel for a few hours before dark. I scrambled to get things done, and arrived at the funnel later than I had hoped to. To top things off, I had forgotten to put my clean hunting clothes in the truck that morning. I considered canning the hunt, and going home, after all I was late, and now had to hunt in my stinky work clothes. That seemed to be the way my luck was running this season. I'd be lying if I said I wasn't slightly discouraged as I trudged off toward the old hemlock tree, but the outdoors was teaching me lessons about perseverance.

Instead of the muzzleloader, I had the scoped 30-30 that my grandfather had given me, which is also the gun that I killed my first deer with. I couldn't help but notice the lack of deer sign, as I made my way in, so it's no surprise that I did not have huge hopes. I shielded myself against the wind as I settled in against the hemlock tree with an hour and a half of day light left. Windy conditions aren't the best to hunt in, but I kept my eyes peeled any way.

About 20 minutes had gone by when the steady rhythmic footfalls of a running deer became audible. The dry leaves told me that it wasn't bounding, but rather running at a steady trot. Unfortunately, with the wind blowing, and swirling, I could not tell what direction the deer was approaching from, but the sound was getting loud enough that I knew it was definitely going to be visible soon. With senses on full alert, I scanned the area trying to pinpoint what direction the deer was coming from, all the while hoping that it was not approaching from behind. I finally caught movement out in front of me. The deer ran down a small knoll and stopped about 40 yards away. The problem was that he stopped directly behind enough brush that I could not see anything but his head which sported a nice set of antlers I might add. His headgear only added to the heart pounding anticipation. I think the buck must have smelled me, and this is why he came to such a sudden stop. With the wind blowing, and swirling, I don't think he could figure out from which direction the danger was coming from. So he stood there for what seemed like an eternity.

I pulled my rifle just ahead of him into the opening where his head was protruding. The opening was small — between two trees that prevented me from seeing the entire length of the deer all at once. If he continued straight ahead on the same course, he would cross this opening, and it would be my only chance at a shot as there was thick brush on the other side of the opening as well. I had the hammer cocked and my finger on the trigger with my elbows locked into my knees. I could see the buck's head in the edge of my scope as I tried to level my crosshairs in the center of the opening at about the height the buck's chest should be. I was praying for just a couple more steps when it happened. He didn't take the couple of steps I was hoping for, but instead broke directly into the trot again. He was through the opening in a split second, and I was so focused and concentrating I had entered what I call "the zone" for the first time as a hunter. I was so focused that I never heard the crack of the rifle or felt the kick in my shoulder, but as that buck's shoulder streamed by my crosshairs, I had surely let her rip. What I heard next was the clinking and snap cracking of the bucks antlers busting brush as he bounded away making giant leaps.

After the shot I started to shake a little, I sat there and replayed the events in my head for about ten minutes while I regained my composure. I got up and began to scour the area for blood where the deer had been, but to no avail. Everything had happened so quickly, I began to have doubts as to whether my shot had been on or not. I could clearly see where the buck had taken his first big bound as the leaves were all scattered and blown out, but clearly there was no blood.

I began to panic slightly as the reality of a second miss in the same season began to sink in. This couldn't be happening to me, and surely not with a nice buck at stake. I wouldn't be able to sleep for a month. The point where the buck had made his first big jump was not all that far from where he had been when the shot rang out, so I began to circle through the small jack firs to see if I could find where he had come down, and hopefully a nice smattering of blood. I did find where the buck had landed, and again jumped as the leaves were again all blown out from the impact. It was almost a surprising distance he had covered with a single jump. The problem was that there was still no blood, and now my heart really began to sink. You want to talk about one dejected young hunter.

By the time I found where the deer had next landed, and still not a stitch of blood to be seen, I was pretty well convinced that I had missed again. I continued to make small circles in the thick fir trees, and zig zag back and forth until I would again locate the bounding buck's tracks. I kept pacing back and forth looking for the next set of tracks mostly out of frustration, and disbelief, and not knowing what else to do. Still no blood, I was one low hunter, and was very close to just heading back to the truck to wallow in my misery.

When I pushed my way through some fir trees into what appeared to be an opening for me to look for the next set of tracks, there was one very dead seven-point buck laying in front of me. He was all piled up, and judging from the skid marks in the leaves appeared to have died in mid flight, and hit the ground to skid to his final resting place. Now you want to talk about one excited young hunter! The exhilaration and relief boiled to the surface, and I can say it's probably as excited as I've been on a hunt. The low feelings of dejection that led up to the success of finding the buck made it ten times as exhilarating as if the buck had just fallen over dead in his tracks. I went from the lowest of lows to the highest of highs. I gave thanks as I sat there admiring that deer's rack in my hands, and I felt like the luckiest hunter in the world. You know how the saying goes, the sweet isn't so sweet without the bitter.

These were trying times, and there were a lot of uncertainty's in life, such as my parent's going through a divorce, and the anxiety of being out of high school and out on my own. Despite whatever was going on in my personal life, I was on cloud nine for weeks, and, truthfully, for the whole winter as well. What a great success for a young hunter. I spent the whole winter reflecting on that hunt, and basking in the warm cozy feeling of success every time I opened up a package of venison.

The outdoor experience is truly good for the soul. The high protein, and low fat of the venison is good for the body. The lessons learned in the outdoor classroom will make you a better person, teach you how to be successful in life, and help you overcome life's obstacles. Just during this hunting season alone, I learned about patience in waiting for a good shot, and how perseverance, and persistence can pay off even when there's almost no hope while tracking the buck. These good qualities once learned can be applied to all aspects of life. So in short, the whole experience will bring you closer to God.

"Look deep into nature and then you will understand everything better"

~Albert Einstein

In recalling that hunt, I'd say the buck had traveled 75 yards after the shot. I could not find a bullet hole in the deer at the time, and still no blood even where the buck had landed. While gutting out the buck, I found that I had made a perfect shot just behind the shoulder, and had put a bullet hole through the center of the buck's heart. Later while skinning the buck, I found the bullet just under the skin on the opposite shoulder. This is why I always like to have an exit wound. If there had been an exit wound, that buck would have painted the forest red. After traveling through the animal the bullet expands, and leaves a gaping hole on the other side which allows the blood to flow freely onto the ground. This is why I've come to be a fan of the 30-06. When hit properly with the 06, if the animal doesn't fall over in its tracks, there is little doubt as to where he went because there will be a generous amount of blood to follow. The 30-30 punched a nice neat little hole through the bucks heart where the 06 would have blown it apart, it just leaves a devastating wound channel. I'm for sure a fan of using enough gun. Will the 30-30 get the job done? Yup. Will the 30-06 do it better? Yup.

After dragging the buck to my truck, I drove to my dad's house to show him, as it was on the way to the checking station anyway. It was well after dark by the time I reached the checking station, and one of the guys that gathered to see what I had in the back of my truck thought it was a real nice buck until he noticed that one of the brow tines was missing. There was only a nub where the tine should have grown, but did not, and he remarked that this was rather unlucky, and that it should have been an eight point. My reply was that I thought seven was a real lucky number.

> *"When it comes time to die, be not like those whose hearts are filled with the fear of death, so when their time comes they weep and pray for a little more time to live their lives over again in a different way. Sing your death song and die like a hero going home."*
>
> *~ Chief Aupumut Mohican*

> *The previous quote is as much about living as it is about dying. Live out your days in a way that you might be proud, and be satisfied that your days were not wasted*
>
> *~ J.W. Sargent*

2

THE FORKHORN'S HEMLOCK

"Dad you listening? Hey, dad, do you have your ears on?" A bit of static crackled over the two-way radio, and then dad's hushed voice came back over, "Yeah, Josh, go ahead." "I think I hit one, but I might have a bit of trouble finding it." "That was you that shot this morning?" "Yep, it sure was," I replied. "Well where are you? I'll come and give you a hand." "Have you found

13

that bog yet," I asked? "No, but I think I see an opening in the trees that could be it." "Well, give me a call back when you make your way to the edge of it, and I'll come down and get you."

The public land where we hunt in New Hampshire produces approximately, (at least for me personally) on average four deer sightings per year. It's a month long season. Some years I see more, and some years less. Out of those four sightings, I'm lucky to get one or two reasonable shot opportunities. Many years of failure have taught me to hone my skills, and make good on the chances I do get, because it's quite likely I won't get another.

There's a sense of pride, and accomplishment in having my venison packaged, and stacked neatly in the freezer for the coming winter. It's the same kind of warm cozy feeling that you get from sitting next to a warm crackling fire, and peering out of the frosted window panes through the blowing snow and frigid cold of a nor'easter, and admiring your winter's fire wood, cut, split, and neatly stacked. Besides, when I hear that question that I know is coming every year — "Hey Josh dya getch ya deeya?" I want to be able to say, yup. For me the sight of a hemlock tree will conjure up all these images, the sights and smells of deer season, and, before you know it, I'm reliving hunts past, and anticipating those to come.

The hemlock tree is easily my favorite tree in the forest. I've killed more deer out from under hemlock trees than any other. Most tree's foliage grows up toward the sun, but the hemlock's branches sweep down toward the ground. It's for this reason that a hemlock tree makes such an excellent natural blind. Just nestle in against the trunk of the tree, and break off any low sweeping branches that might interfere with shooting. Not only do the low sweeping branches break up your outline, they also naturally shed water, and snow. There's been many a time I've nestled into the comforting shelter of a hemlock to wait out weather, or eat my lunch.

Most fir, and spruce trees have a pleasant aroma when their needles are crushed, but there's none sweeter than that of a hemlock. A few hemlock boughs tossed into a plastic bin with your hunting clothes makes for an excellent cover scent. My favorite deer stand is located in a hemlock. Nothing symbolizes the great north woods more than a stately old hemlock, and they are even prettier when their branches are heavy with snow.

That being said, the morning of the forkhorns' hemlock, dad and I parked the truck at a new area. As dad killed the motor, I jumped out of the truck into the early morning quiet. We had wanted to try deer hunting in this area for several years. It is a ways from where we live, and we had never actually set foot in this piece of woods. We got our muzzleloaders out of their cases with the help of flashlights, as the nocturnal rhythms of nature had yet to give way to even a hint of light. We had a hunch there could be some good deer hunting in this place, and muzzleloader season would provide a chance to prove that theory one way or the other.

Overly eager to get going, and in an attempt to rush the sun's early morning chore, dad started up an old tote road, and I headed at a 90-degree-angle straight into the woods. I hadn't gotten very far when I encountered some of that wonderful boot sucking muck. After much struggling, and frustration, as it was just about impossible to be quiet, I finally found some high ground. I felt as though I had probably scared away anything within half a mile, but that's one of the things you deal with when you're still unfamiliar with an area.

I continued along quietly until I found the reason for the wet muck, I was out on a peninsula in the middle of a bog. I felt as though I was backtracking, but I worked my way around, and thought if I could get to the other side, I'd have a decent sized piece of woods to explore. The land had seemed fairly flat, and monotonous, but as I approached the other side of the bog, I encountered some ridges, and with them came an interesting feeling of luck. I couldn't put my finger on exactly what it was, but my deer hunter's instinct started telling me that things were looking a little better.

As I started up over the first decent sized hardwood ridge, a deer trail could be seen paralleling it half way up through the leaves. It was starting to get light in good shape by now, and as I followed the path through the cut up leaves, it turned up and over the ridge. I was creeping along slowly, the freshly fallen leaves seemed to be piled six inches deep, and were aggravatingly crunchy.

Trying to be as quiet as possible, I shuffled along with both hands on my muzzleloader. Just as I crested the ridge I thought, "man this is really startin to get hawny (that's new England for horny) looking." The thought no sooner went through my head when at least two deer exploded out of a small hollow about 50 yards out in front of me. I pulled my gun just in time to catch the white of a tail through my scope bounding out of sight. I was caught out in the open, and the cover of a hemlock tree, almost strategically placed amongst the otherwise bare hardwoods, looked awfully tempting, but it was 20 yards to my left. In my early years of hunting, I know I would have made for that tree, and sat down to watch for a while, but something, most likely experience, told me to stay put. I slowly hunkered down to one knee, and scanned the open hardwoods that dropped into the small ravine in front of me. "Come on, something else is going to come through, I can feel it." After what seemed like a long time, I heard leaves slowly start crunching off to my right. It wasn't long before I started to see patches of brown moving through the leaf work.

As the deer approached, I was already down on one knee, but I flattened myself even more against the ground to lower my profile as I was in the wide open. The deer was only 30 yards away, and I already had my muzzleloader on my shoulder, and rested on my knee, but felt I needed to be aimed a little more to the right in order to be lined up when the deer finally stepped into the clear. It was awkward, but I successfully managed to shift my weight, and position myself correctly. As I made the adjustment, I made a small amount of noise, and the deer instantly stopped, and keyed in on my position. I froze perfectly still except for the end of my muzzleloader rocking back, and forth to the steady hammering of my heart.

There was no shot available as there was a blow down between us. I noticed, as I sat there peering over the top of my scope, how well the deer, only 30 yards away blended into its surroundings. The animal was almost invisible to me except for the small patch of white around his nose that I was focused on. The stand off lasted for a good long while, and I felt it could go either way. There was a small bit of relief as he slowly started to walk forward instead of bolting. As he proceeded forward there were several moments when I thought I could have taken a shot, and even once I started to put the squeeze on the trigger, but ended up letting off. I only had one shot, and wanted it to count. Just as he came into the wide open he turned to face me, and still I held off for a preferable side shot.

He actually started to take a few steps toward me, I think out of curiosity, but then started acting really uneasy. He turned to his right a little, and presented me with a quartering-on shot which I took as soon as my crosshairs settled on the front of the shoulder. Judging by his body language, I think that small turn, and flicker of the tail he made would have been followed by a whirl, and a bound toward safety. In the instant after the shot, and looking through the scope, I could still see that deer mule kick through the haze of the muzzleloader's smoke, just before my vision was completely clouded by the thick plume as it bellowed out into the early morning air. The smell of burnt powder in the crisp air of a New England fall morning filled my nostrils, and I strained to see around it as the smoke drifted up through the suns first rays of orange light.

Thinking back I can almost see myself from above, with the brim of my hat rolled back and my one shot, plastered against the earth amongst the leaves on that hardwood ridge like a predator crouched, and ready to pounce, as the smoke rolled out the end of my barrel in that unmistakable muzzleloader kapoof!

There are no huge secrets how I was able to get a shot at this deer. A few years ago, it would have been just another story of "one that got away." First off, like I said, I would have gone to the hemlock tree for cover, and in doing so spooked any deer still left in the area, secondly, I may have gotten over eager, and taken my one shot before a good shot presented itself, and finally, I had the patience to hold off on a frontal shot, watch the deer's body language, and shoot at just the right time as the deer quartered, and before he bolted. In many cases

The forkhorn's hemlock buck.

it's the attention to the small details that often makes the difference between success, and failure.

I heard the deer go crashing down over the ridge. I knelt there reloading, my breathing heavy, and trying to steady my shaking hands a little bit as I poured the powder down the barrel, the air was still, and the muzzleloader smoke just kind of hung all around me like a fog. I saw just the back of a deer skedaddling off to the right partway down the ridge. I thought it to be the deer I had shot at. Reloaded, I made my way over to where the buck had been standing. I was shocked that I didn't find any blood sign.

After much searching, I finally found the small tuft of hair that I knew was there, and confirmed a hit. I proceeded in the direction that the deer had taken, and surprisingly not a drop of blood was to be found. I went directly over to the side of the ridge where I had seen the deer run, and still no blood. After looking the area over a little bit I went back up to the hemlock, and took a seat to wait, and think things over carefully. I just knew that I had hit that deer solid, and the way he mule kicked just reinforced that belief. That's when I came to the conclusion the deer I had seen after the shot must have been a fourth deer.

That marks the first time I've ever seen four deer in New Hampshire before sunrise was complete. I just sat there for an hour, and finished watching the sunrise. Partly because I wanted to give the deer time, and partly because I didn't want to disturb dad so early in the hunt, but mostly just to savor the anticipation a little longer, and that leads me back to my opening paragraph.

"Hey, Josh, if you can hear me, I'm at the edge of that bog." "Yeah, dad, I hear ya, I just found my deer." "What is it?" "A nice looking forkhorn I replied, hang on I'll be right down to get ya." Shortly after getting up from beneath the hemlock tree, I found my buck dead within 100 yards, and waiting against a hemlock tree of his own. I found the nice little 140-pound forkhorn laying in a small depression formed by a gnarled portion of the tree's root, his butt stuck up in the air from being piled up on top of himself. It appeared as if he had died in mid stride. I was curious about my hit as there was not a stitch of blood to be found. The bullet had entered the front shoulder, and gone right through the boiler room, and stopped under the hide on the opposite shoulder. There was no exit wound so no blood.

I suppose, when it comes right down to it, we're all just waiting under the hemlock.

**Another forkhorn taken from the area later in the season.
His deer was also taken with a muzzleloader.**

3

CARIBOU HUNT JUSTIFICATION

Before I get into the caribou hunts, I'd like to talk a little about the money aspect of the hunt, and getting the best bang for the buck (no pun intended). If you can ever get it together to go caribou hunting, I highly recommend it. For me, it was a life changing experience. To hunt in a true wilderness untouched, and unspoiled is something that words cannot describe. It has to be experienced.

I once was watching an outdoor hunting special, and I forget who the TV personality was that hosted the show, but I remember one thing he said because it makes me think of my first caribou. He said that on his first ever caribou hunt he had shot a small caribou bull. Most of the guys back home after seeing the picture said, "man I'd never shoot a small caribou like that." Then he went on to say that "most of the guys back home were right, because most of the guys back home never went on a caribou hunt."

I was fishing with a friend, and my upcoming caribou hunt naturally came up in conversation. He said that he would love to go on a hunt like that, but his finances just wouldn't allow it. He even went so far as to poke a little fun at me about being wealthy. Later when we were done fishing he jumped into his 40 thousand dollar full size decked out pick-up truck that came with a full size payment, and I got into my paid for, little four cylinder Nissan beater with 220 thousand miles on it. I had considered getting a new truck that year, but I could justify a caribou hunt a lot easier if I didn't. It was an easy decision, the truck had 255 thousand miles on it when I dumped it the following year, and I had some great memories of an awesome caribou hunt. I shot a large doe one year, and a few of the guys thought it fitting to poke fun at me, and say that the doe wasn't all that big, but my truck was just really little. I have to admit, when they all jumped into their full size trucks, I felt a twinge of jealousy. There are a lot of people that use money as an excuse not to go on a caribou hunt, but I think that if you truly desire to do something it can be accomplished. We all have priorities, and I'm willing to make sacrifices so that I can do some of these hunts that I've always dreamt about.

That being said, I have a job that involves physical labor, so the money comes through sweat and hard work. It doesn't matter how you twist it, a caribou hunt is not cheap, and I don't take expenditures such as a caribou hunt lightly. One question that I seem to hear a lot is, "what if after spending all that money, you don't get one?" With fair chase hunting that is always a possibility. As long as I've hunted as hard as I could, and to the utmost of my ability the sting of failure doesn't hurt all that bad. Besides it's not all about money. A caribou hunt is an adventure with float planes, and snow storms, and unspoiled wilderness, bears, wolves, the northern lights, reel smoking pike, beautiful brook trout, and caribou with huge gnarly racks, how could you feel cheated after an experience like that? I'm in it for the adventure as much as the kill.

I'm not being financially rewarded by Jack Hume Adventures for writing this. I researched all the different hunts quite extensively before throwing down a deposit. Jack Hume Adventures is what I settled on, and the research paid off. After all, this very book is named after, and inspired by a hunt that Jack Hume Adventures provided for me. That in itself speaks volumes. In Montreal you get to spend time with a lot of other hunters hunting with a whole variety of different outfitters. Through discussions with other hunters, and hearing some of the stories they had been through, I couldn't help but feel as though I had a top notch experience with Jack Hume Adventures. Richard Hume (Jack's son), and his wife Amanda now own and run the outfit. It's a family run business, and Richard is there to see you off when you leave on the float plane, and he's there when you return. Some other outfits will have a front man, and you never get to talk to the owner, or the real person running the show, and oftentimes complaints fall on deaf ears in a situation like that. Richard is there because as a hard-working business man, he knows how hard you work for your money, and he cares about providing a quality experience. He's going to be there at the conclusion of the hunt to look you in the eye, and hear any complaints or praise that you have. In other words, he isn't hiding behind a front man.

On my first hunt a lot of the other outfitters were backed up due to weather delays, and hunters were spending time way laid in Schefferville. Schefferville is a small Indian village in northern Canada that is a jumping-off point for many of the Caribou hunts. The only way to reach Schefferville is by railroad or airplane. From Schefferville hunters are flown out even further into the Canadian bush by float plane to hunt. Despite the other outfitters delays, Richard had our group of hunters out the very day we got to Schefferville. On my second hunt, with fuel costs sky rocketing, he flew us 200 miles to his furthest camp north to insure our best chances at filling our tags. Would a lesser outfitter have dumped you in a closer camp with fewer caribou to keep costs down? I don't know, but I wouldn't take the chance. The last thing that I would like to mention is that at least one year that I know of Richard called his last group of hunters for the year, and told them that they weren't seeing many caribou, and that they were welcome to come, but they might do better punching tags if they came the following year. How many outfitters do you think would do that? From a business standpoint, that's giving up a lot of money. Another outfitter may have had you come so they could make the money knowing full well that your chances at success were slim. These are just a few of the instances that have occurred that have convinced me Richard truly cares, and is interested in providing a quality experience. I really feel as though Jack Hume Adventures went the extra mile in a lot of areas to provide a great hunt. It's for these reasons that Jack Hume Adventures boasts the highest amount of repeat customer business in the industry. That alone should tell the story. It's a rare occasion when you can't think of some aspect of a hunting experience to complain about, or offer advice for improvements, but that was my experience with Jack Hume Adventures. I experienced a degree of excellence that I've never experienced on a guided hunt anywhere else. It's also worth noting that I hunted with Jack Hume Adventures long before I had written a book or received any notoriety for writing. I wasn't pampered or treated special, I was just the average hunter coming through. It's for all of these reasons that I feel comfortable recommending, and putting my seal of approval on the Jack Hume experience. For any further information, checking out the Jack Hume website would be the way to go. A caribou hunt is as close to God that you can get and still be alive. Learn more about him at http://www.jackhumeadventures.com.

4

FIRST CARIBOU

Why don't you go someplace warm and tropical? It's half the price. Relax down in the Caribbean as the sun gently warms you to sleep. Close your eyes and let all your fears melt away while the warm damp sand gently squishes through your toes, and the sound of the ocean waves caressing the beach carry you off into a careless dreamlike sleep.

I questioned my own sanity as I flew over the frozen tundra. I not only came here, but paid dearly to do so. The tundra below appeared to be a vast wasteland for as far as the eye could see. Nothing, but black spruce, and tamarack —

streams and rivers connecting bogs, ponds and lakes. The normally vast view was rendered short due to the light, but steady snow that flew out of the ten-degree cold and barraged the float plane.

The far north is mesmerizing. The land is cold, and rugged, it's picturesque landscape has a draw that lures you in. The land is filled with the unknown, and the wonder of what lies beyond. The hills have caribou hidden in their shadows, and the rivers have brilliantly colored brook trout lurking beneath their dark currents.

The Canadian bush can be a beautiful place.

What truly draws me to this place. Simply put: FEAR. The fear of the unknown and becoming hopelessly lost in a wilderness that is wild, vast, impossible to walk out of, and nearly impossible to live in year round.

Forty-five minutes into the flight, the plane crested a ridge, and a lake with a tiny plywood shack on its shore came into view. This was to be home for the next eight days. The plane set down on the water, and I went about settling into camp and becoming acquainted with the other hunters, the camp manager, and the cook. After a large home cooked meal, and plenty of hunting stories, we all drifted to sleep with large caribou bulls dancing in our dreams.

Morning came quickly, and before I knew it, freezing sleet and rain were pelting me in the face as I was being motored to the opposite end of the lake in an aluminum boat for the day's hunt. I stepped out of the boat on a sandy beach littered with caribou tracks, and watched as the boat slowly grew smaller, and the fading drone of the motor gave way to an unexplainable silence.

I walked to the end of the beach, and stepped into the Canadian bush. Thank god for rubber boots, it's a wet, often thick and boggy land covered in slippery moss, and lichen. The next hour was spent slowly still hunting along the lake's outlet, a fierce raging torrent of whitewater some 75 yards wide. I cleared out a small hole in the thick underbrush along the edge of the river where I had a decent view up and down the shoreline, and climbed in. I sat there methodically scanning the shoreline while I ate my lunch. The wet was starting to seep in around the edges of my cheap rain suit, and I was starting to wonder if finding a caribou in this vast wilderness was going to be possible, and then it happened. I caught a flicker of movement across the river. With a small dose of adrenaline, my heart beat a little quicker, and I strained to see the whole animal. With the steady rain the woods were in a haze-like mist that wasn't quite a fog, but made it difficult to see. I kept catching movement, and a glimpse of white here, and there through the spruce trees. The animal was slowly headed up river. I dropped everything except my gun, and crawled on hands, and knees away from the river back into the bush. When I felt I was a safe distance, I stood up, and ran up river 75 yards or so, then carefully crawled back to the river edge. Now thoroughly soaked, and covered in mud with rain dripping down over my nose, I, again, tried to spot movement. After a few tense moments of searching the caribou finally stepped into the clear. I got my first good look at an animal standing before me that I had previously only seen in pictures or video. It was a smaller bull, that at first I was inclined to pass on. It kept offering perfect shot angles though, and my meat hunter ways eventually won out, I decided this would work for my first caribou. I did after all have a second tag.

My first caribou, a small bull. Notice how my wool hat is plastered down over my head due to the soaking wet conditions

As I put my scope to my eye, I soon realized that I couldn't see a thing. The lenses were fogged on the outside, and covered in water droplets. I quickly tried to clear the lenses with my undershirt as I knelt in the waist high underbrush, but my shirt was soaked, and only served to smear around the watery mess. I put the scope to my eye again, and was eventually, by some stroke of luck, able to locate the animal, though just barely, through the fog of the scope. The brush I was kneeling in was just high enough so that I couldn't use my knee for a rest, and still see through it. I didn't dare stand for fear of being detected, so I was forced to shoot offhand in a kneeling position. My crosshairs finally found the bulls shoulder, and the rifle roared. I immediately chambered another round, and when again I located the bull, he was hunched up, and stumbling forward a bit. All I could see was the bull's neck, and when I fired he dropped from view. The caribou was roughly 100 yards distant and across the river. The hundreds of rounds I had burned through my rifle all summer had just satisfyingly paid off with a difficult shot, and a humane kill.

I made my way back to the lake edge, and called Brian my camp manager on the two-way radio, as I would have to be ferried to the other side of the river mouth. The job of boning, and packing my caribou was made easier with Brian's help. His hand is well trained with the knife after having performed the task hundreds of times.

While transporting the caribou to the boat, I had on several occasions encountered a group of spruce grouse. I don't think the group of birds had ever seen a human before as they would allow you to approach within six feet of them before flying a short distance to another branch. I started to think a couple of spruce grouse would taste good with my caribou dinner that evening, but was afraid my 30/06 would probably leave me with little but feathers to eat. I found a nice stout stick about two feet long. Considering I was able to approach the birds within throwing distance, and after much trying, I was eventually able to make good on two of them. The camp cook made a delicious grouse stew that complemented the caribou steak dinner nicely.

Though not a tropical paradise the far north is instead rugged, and hard, but as is often the case "hard" usually has its rewards, and this time was no exception. I would not have traded the experience for all the sandy beaches in the Caribbean.

If you eat like a wild man you may start to hunt like a wild man. This spruce grouse fell victim to the author and his throwing stick.

5

CARIBOU MOUNTAIN HIGH

I was on a ridge top leaning against a Volkswagen-sized rock. I had foregone hunting down around the lake as I had the two previous days. The views were spectacular up here. I had hiked high above the northern Quebec bush where the wind was fierce. I could see camp down on the lake one mile distant.

The view from the float plane.
No roads, but pure wilderness for as far as the eye can see.

I scanned the ridges surrounding me through binoculars, and would then look at what I could see with the naked eye in front of me. Suddenly a cow caribou emerged from the rocky outcropping in front of me. She walked a course that would follow by at about 50 yards to my right, but she spotted me, and cut down into some black spruce, and swamp to my left. Another cow, and a small bull followed her course. Several minutes passed, and I resumed glassing the ridges around me. When I looked back at the last spot where I had seen the caribou disappear, there, as if out of thin air, stood the caribou of my dreams. A few moments later, and I may have missed knowing he was there at all. He was literally a few seconds from disappearing on the same course as the cows and smaller bull had gone earlier. Antlers reaching toward the heavens, and half-rubbed velvet dangling from them, it was the most gnarly looking massive mess I had ever seen looming above an animal's head. I knew quicker than the blink of an eye he was a shooter, and was about to disappear just as quickly. I struggled to find him in the crosshairs some 125 yards below me.

I had booked my hunt through Jack Hume Adventures one year previously. I booked the "hunt on your own" hunt because it was cheaper, I'm a man of meager means — I carve wood for a living, and I'm somewhat of a loner anyway. There were five hunters in camp besides myself — a group of three, and another group of two. The group of two was a retired lifetime marine and an explosives expert. When they told me I was "adventurous for traveling all this way and hunting on my own," I began to wonder myself. If you get turned around up here, it can easily turn into a death sentence.

This is a land untouched by man, where caribou, wolves and bear roam, and not much else. There is no air, water, or noise pollution caused by man. The silence is deafening, and you drink straight from the lake, or whatever stream is handy. Words cannot explain this almost religious experience. I can tell you all day, but as I said before if you ever have the chance, please experience this for yourself.

Camp life was excellent, my camp manager Brian, was responsible for keeping firewood stocked, and for ferrying six hunters around the lake to whatever vantage point they might choose to hunt from. His wife Cindy was responsible for cooking meals for eight and keeping camp tidy. They both did an exceptional job. I've never seen pie crusts put together, and home made bread made from scratch with such ease. It goes without saying the meals were out of this world! They both come from Labrador down on the coast where they travel by snow machine in the winter.

Most times hunting camps are not all that fancy. This one was warm, and it was dry, and therefore it was a palace as far as this hunter was concerned.

33

I noticed a 220 conibear in Brian's personal effects, and inquired about it. The 220 was for marauding martin who attacked the meat house in caribou camp. It turns out, Brian runs an extensive trap line each winter back home in Labrador. We talked trapping in the evenings, and I was surprisingly able enough to give this seasoned trapper a piece of advice about trapping otter that he found interesting.

I had nagged Brian about hunting the ridge the first two days in camp, and he just as quickly discouraged me from it. In his thick Canadian accent, he would say, "No hunters go up dare." I had taken a small bull around a river mouth on the second day of the hunt. There was no keeping me off that ridge the third day. I was dropped off on the opposite side of the lake to hike the ridge on the third morning. After an hour and a half I attained the summit of the land, I was overtaken by what God has allowed me in this life, to witness such a beautiful and pristine land just the way His hand created it, everything covered in moss and lichen. On the inside of our small hunting shack's door was written a short poem: "I sit upon a mountain high, with the black spruce, the lichen, and the black fly. This is no place for me and you, for this is the land of the caribou." I'm convinced that whoever wrote the poem was surely inspired by the same view I took in on this mountaintop.

I've heard it said, "modern civilization is just a tiny blip in time since early man first rubbed two sticks together." Being in this land made me realize the truth in this statement. Some people look at me like I'm an oddball for killing and butchering my own meat when really the opposite is true. Anyone who is close to the land, and partakes first hand in the food chain, will eventually experience a feeling of satisfaction that cannot be described. Some people don't realize the need to be in tune with the natural world around them. I've heard talk of the meaning of life, and I just don't think it gets any better than the peace and satisfaction of a good clean conscience, and knowing you're in the right. You eventually need to realize the primal urge to be a part of the food chain.

Blaaaaam! I squeezed the trigger, and the old monarch nailed the ground as if hit with a ton of bricks. I was on my feet, and back on my butt again five yards to my right with a new 30/06 round chambered, and trained on the bou again from this better vantage point. All I saw through the scope were hooves flailing for a short moment, and then all was still. Before rising to my feet, I called Brian on the two way radio, and told him I had just knocked over a big bull. It had been a slow week of hunting thus far, and his reply over the static choked radio was an exciting, "you're the man!" and I'll be there in about an hour and a half to help you process, and pack out the meat, antlers and cape. As an amateur taxidermist, the skin from the head and neck, also known as the cape, along with the antlers was going to be my first big game head mount. I started processing the bull, and immediately had company on this lonely ridge top. Canadian jays, also known as "whiskey jacks" appeared from the ridge top tundra. They have little fear of man, will often eat from your hand, and are said to be the reincarnated souls of old woodsmen.

A couple of Canadian jays also known as whiskey jacks. They were the only company the author had after killing a caribou as he hunted on a ridge top one mile distant from camp

On the way down the mountain, stressed with the heavy burden of full packs, Brian was leading the way. We had made our way from the open tundra back down into the bush. Antlers draped about my shoulders, Brian poked through the thick brush, and said, "oh sheet, this is the last piece of ground God created, and He must have been in a bad mood." It was then I realized why he had discouraged me from hunting the ridge, and also that I was the guy in that adventure I had read about in so many outdoor magazine articles.

The end of the week had come too quickly. I had killed my two caribou and caught brook trout the length of my elbow to my fingertips, fiery red with spots. It had been a slow week of hunting. Only a couple of other smallish caribou had been shot. The other hunters eyeballed my caribou rack with a look of envy, and a few jokingly threatened me with bodily harm. As the floatplane landed, I got down on all fours, push up style at the lake edge, and sucked in one last belly full of that clean clear water. I reluctantly boarded the floating otter, I felt the engines roar to life, and rev up, the plane began to throttle forward. I vowed to return to this magical land once again.

Brian meets a float plane coming into camp to fly out meat.

As I sit here in New Hampshire, I close my eyes. I can feel the sensation of not wanting to get out of my warm sleeping bag to step out into the frigid predawn Quebec darkness to relieve myself. But as I step out of the cabin at 1:00 A.M. I find my shade from the northern lights in the shadow of a black spruce. I can still see them dancing across, and illuminating the night sky. I can hear wolves howling in the distance, and I forget all about the cold sting in the air that bites at me. Tonight I'm celebrating booking my hunt next year with a fat juicy caribou steak.

Sometimes going the extra mile in life doesn't always pay off, but more often than not it does. In this case going the extra mile (literally) made the difference for the author as he was able to harvest this trophy caribou on a ridge top one mile distant from camp.

> *"The first peace, which is the most important, is that which comes within the souls of people when they realize their relationship, their oneness with the universe and all its powers, and when they realize that at the center of the universe dwells the Great Spirit, and that this center is really everywhere, it is within each of us"*
>
> *~ Black Elk Oglala Sioux*

6

COLD SOULS

I could hardly believe that a year had gone by so quickly. Here I was on my way to Montreal once again — destination caribou land. This time, with my father by my side, we barreled northbound up the New Hampshire/Vermont border. My tales of the northland, and awesome adventure from my solo caribou hunt the year before had proven irresistible for him.

We met the other four guys that were to be our bunk mates for the week to come at the airport. They seemed to be a decent bunch of guys at first observation, and proved to be so in the coming days. Upon arriving in Schefferville, I confirmed that we were going to have the same hard-working camp manager and cook from the previous year, Brian and Cindy. I also learned that they were in the furthest camp north of Schefferville, which carried the name Coursoulles. Pronounced Core-souls. As we looked at the wall size map in Jack Hume's office, there was nothing but wilderness for 350 Miles north to Ungava bay. Colored pins represented the 28 camps that Jack Hume Adventures has spread across this great wilderness. Way above the cluster of the other pins to the north, and off all by itself like an old loner was a black pin almost off the map. Beside it read "Coursoulles."

Soaring toward our destination, as excited as we were, it was useless to try and talk above the ear cracking pop of the float plane's motor. So each hunter, including myself, was plastered to the window, in awe, absorbing the serene beauty of the northern Canadian bush as it passed below, each of us left to our own thoughts. Somewhere swallowed up in all those spruce trees and lake-peppered tundra was a caribou with my name on it.

As I sat there on our 200-mile trek due north, a conversation that I had with Cindy the previous winter came flooding back to me. She had returned from her cooking job to her home down on the coast near Newfoundland, and crafted for me a hand made quilt with polar bears on it. Words cannot describe the beauty imparted in this work of art, and as for warmth, I think the polar bears would be jealous. I called to thank her after receiving it in the mail, and she told me a story of almost getting stuck in Jack Humes furthest camp North during the last week of the caribou hunt. They were snowed in, and the weather was relentless snow, and freezing conditions. Due to her Canadian accent, at the time I thought she said the camp they were in were cold souls. Being that it was the furthest camp north the name seemed fitting. She said the pilot had flown the last five miles through a snow storm to get them out. The pilot who was sent to snatch them out of the cold icy clutches of the north's harsh winds and snow, was one of the most experienced pilots operating out of Schefferville, and is employed by Jack Hume Adventures. After the pilot whisked them into the air, he offered the reassurance that in five miles the snow would subside, though I can't imagine that it was much consolation at the time. These bush pilots operate by sight, and a heavy snow is no condition to be flying in. I'm sure that uneasy cold fear that grips your soul was alive and well inside that plane on that blustery day. Brian and Cindy surely thought of there children as they were so close to returning home after being away for so long, but when the pilot turned back and asked Cindy if she was scared the brave little lady said, "No." It began to dawn on me that the destination our plane was bearing down on was this very place.

Before I knew it, we were helping the hunters who had been in camp the previous week load their antlers, our gear already stowed safely on the beach. All six hunters had successfully tagged two bulls each. As each rack passed through my hands down the assembly line toward the plane, the anticipation built a little more. The parting hunters' advice to the just arriving hunters was, "wait for the big ones." For some of the guys, I think buck fever had already started to set in.

It didn't take long, after introducing my dad to Brian and Cindy, to climb into our hunting clothes. We had a few hours of daylight left, and intended on making good use of it. After some quick directions from Brian, we were headed straight uphill, behind the camp, to a blind that he had built at the peak of the land out on the open tundra. It was a one-quarter mile hike to what was to become known as, "the crows nest." It was an excellent vantage point from which to glass, and we soon found that almost all of the 700 migrating caribou we were to see that week, passed by within 200 yards of the nest.

We were in the blind so quickly after getting off the plane that we were almost in shock at the sheer immensity of our wilderness surroundings. Just five hours earlier we had been in the bustling push and shove hustle of Montreal, and now we sat in one of the most remote places a person could be. Soon after directing the other hunters to there locations, Brian was sharing the blind with my father and me. We had been there a good 20 minutes settling in, putting our binoculars to use, and not seeing much but pretty countryside. As soon as Brian's trained eye scoured the land he began to point out caribou here and there that we had not previously seen. Most of them were bedded or milled about, and Brian assured us that as evening approached they would soon be moving past our location. A couple of shots rang out from a ridge to the south. The high-powered rifle sounded as if it were a mere popgun as the shots echoed across, and were swallowed up by the wide-open expanse. Brian left to investigate.

Not long after he disappeared, we saw a group of approximately 18 caribou on a ridge a mile away start in our direction. As they drew closer, that small dose of adrenaline known to all big game hunters, boosted my heart rate to a steady hammering. Could we really be this lucky to have a group of caribou pass by within an hour of getting off the plane? The giant antlers bobbing above the encroaching animals' heads loomed closer still. Just as we started to get a decent look at the animals antlers they disappeared into a fold in the land that appeared flat from where we sat. We decided at that point that dad was going to shoot first because he had yet to kill a caribou, and I had already experienced the hunt of a lifetime the year before. The minutes passed, and I remarked that the animals should have certainly reappeared on the ridge closest to us by now, but the folds in the land were deceiving. I started to lose hope, but my pulse had no sooner returned to normal, and my father half whispered, half hissed, "there they are." I picked out the two largest bulls in the bunch, and when the largest of them stepped out in front of the others, I told dad to take him as soon as he felt comfortable, just don't miss. At 150 yards shooting off hand, the sharp crack of dad's rifle broke the silence. He missed, but promptly shot again. The giant bull went down at the report of the second shot, and I found the next largest bull in my crosshairs who was trotting by now. I gently squeezed the trigger, and watched as the bull continued to run. I was just looking for my second shot when the animal started to wobble a little, I hesitated for a few seconds, and he tipped over. I couldn't believe the scene that had just played out before my very eyes. We had taken an animal so quickly, hunting together, and within seconds of each other. It didn't matter what happened the rest of the week, the hunt had already been made for me.

The remainder of the evening was spent butchering, and packing caribou meat off the hillside. What a sweet chore it was. Darkness, and exhaustion ensued, and the antlers and capes were left on the mountain for the morning. We were the only hunters to score on that first day, the two shots that rang out before ours had both been misses. Sleep came easy that night, and it found me with a big old grin on my face.

The second morning dawned clear and cool. I awoke to anxious hunters scrambling around in the dark looking for stray accessories. I soon joined them, and somebody announced that there were caribou in the lake out in front of camp. Everyone rushed to the door, and sure enough several dark forms could just barely be made out swimming not 150 yards offshore. This increased the intensity of the scramble. We decided to put off packing down our cape and antlers to give somebody else an early morning chance at the crow's nest. As Dad, and I hastily made our way south through the Canadian bush, the early morning dusk was cool on my face, and still not fully awake, I stepped in a hole and about jarred my eye teeth loose. After arriving at our position on a ridge to the south we spread out a couple hundred yards. As soon as I put the binoculars to my eyes the morning cobwebs were instantly gone. Better than a cup of coffee, the approaching herd of caribou contained some better than average

My firsts "Cold Souls" caribou taken shortly after getting off the plane.

Dad's first caribou of the trip. This bull is wide, and has great tops.

bulls. Now fully alert, I watched as the group skirted out of range of me, and proceeded right up over the crow's nest. Through binoculars from one-half mile away, I looked on as the two hunters in the nest dropped a bull each. As we made our way over to admire the hunters' bulls, and finish up our chores from the day before, we heard shots from the ridge north of the crow's nest. The two hunters there had also managed to take a caribou from the bunch.

One-half hour later while helping process animals dad happened to look up and another herd had approached undetected to within 50 yards of us as we were busy with the task at hand. One of the bulls was quite large with a double shovel, and the gunfire that followed brought a successful end to dad's hunt not two hours into the first morning. On my way down the hill, straining under a pack load of meat, I met Brian just making his way up. He remarked that as he lay in bed earlier it sounded like slaughter up on the hill, and wondered if we had demolished the caribou herd. I agreed that he had his work cut out for him, but it wasn't as bad as it sounded as several of the guys had shot multiple times at each animal. There were four animals downed in total.

Dad's second caribou had a nice double shovel.

My second caribou was very symmetrical with palmated tops, and back scratcher points.

Dad displays one of the many northern pike caught.

About midmorning the meat processing chores seemed to be under control, and a steady stream of animals had started to filter from south to north. Dad, Brian and I sat perched in the crow's nest glassing animals, and soon one of the other hunters joined. Brian picked out a bull that he thought was a dandy, and when it closed the 100-yard mark my rifle roared. I chambered another round, and when again I located the animal in my scope, a brilliant blotch of red flowed down over the animals bright white mane from just behind the shoulder. He continued to run, but Brian said don't bother shooting again he's dead on his feet, seconds later the caribou lost his footing and crashed to the tundra. Right after my shot the other hunter had settled on a bull, and as he prepared to shoot, his breathing intensified to such a level that I thought he would hyperventilate. Dad talked him through it, and told him to take slow deep breaths, and concentrate on the shoulder. He made a good shot and the bull dropped very quickly. He instantly grabbed my hand, and vigorously shook it. It was great to see his level of excitement, and to have shared such an experience with him, Brian and my father. Our entire hunting party had tagged out on two bulls each within 48 hours of getting off the plane.

The next couple of days were cold and drizzly, and a thick fog shrouded the lake. The dreary gun metal gray skies reminded me of the November deer season back home, a stark contrast to the bright bluebird skies we had hunted under the first two days. The weather seemed to correspond with and intensify both the high of the hunt, and the kill, and the dreary weather with the anticlimactic realization of two punched caribou tags. We helped Brian put a new roof on the camp, and spent a little time fishing. When we weren't fishing, we'd glass and stalk caribou for the fun of it and to capture some pictures.

The lake where we were had northern pike in it. They proved a formidable match for our light weight little pack rods. I'm more of a trout and salmon fisherman so I wasn't all that excited to wet a line, but nonetheless, dad and I were the first to try our luck. On my fifth or sixth cast, a wake formed behind my lure, and in an explosion of whitewater my little rod was unexpectedly almost ripped from my hands. The reel screamed with torment as the northern peeled out for the other side of the channel. After a short while, and a few more blistering runs, the fish finally came to hand. We were instructed to keep a few for a meal which we did, and as I mentioned before, Cindy cooked beautifully. Brian doesn't even consider the northern pike a fish because it isn't a trout. His distaste was obvious when he wouldn't even look at such an abomination much less touch one. Fish or not, they put up one heck of a stink when enraged with a hook in the corner of their mouth, and I never did tire of summoning those water devils from the depths, and the resulting explosive battle that ensued thereafter.

I came to realize that Brian had his shotgun, which I remembered from the previous year. He also had four shells which he generously handed over to me. The shotgun is a single shot 16 gauge hammer gun that he had left out in the rain the previous year, and when informed of that fact at the dinner table he replied that, "the gun was too old to rust," and continued to eat his dinner. As far as he knows the shotgun is at least 50 years old. I've never heard of the make before, and perhaps somebody could shed some light. On the side of the firearm reads: Cooey Machine and Arms Co., LTD, Coburg, ONT. 32329. He acquired the gun from an old man for the sum of five dollars which is exactly what the old man had paid years prior when he had bought it from an Indian. If wood metal and rust could only talk, what a story this gun would have to tell. I offered Brian to double his money, but the ten dollars wouldn't buy the old girl. I flirted for an afternoon with the gun that was probably close to twice my age in hopes of collecting a spruce grouse or ptarmigan, but as if I was being punished for my youth, and arrogance there were none to be found. The next morning I was sitting down to a big breakfast that Cindy had made when an excited call came over the radio from up on the hill, "Bring the shotgun! Bring the shotgun!" I took off at a trot up the hill gun in tow. When I reached my dad and one of the other hunters, they were hot in pursuit of a ptarmigan with rocks, and sticks. There had been five ptarmigan in total but they had already busted up the birds, and chased them off. The one bird they had followed flushed, and was proving difficult to find. They sent me further up the hill "where the other four birds were." It turned out to be a wild goose chase, and I should have known better as neither of them was interested in staying around to watch, but rather headed down the hill to their hot breakfast. When the other four birds didn't turn up after much scouring of the landscape, I decided to look for the ptarmigan that I had seen flush. I felt I had made amends with the gun, and her shape was starting to feel a little more comfortable in my hands. I was looking in every nook and cranny when from beneath a tangle of black spruce, I caught a flicker of movement which happened to be the birds head bobbing. The well-camouflaged plumage made the bird's shape difficult to discern momentarily, but I soon cocked the hammer and the old 16 swiftly separated the ptarmigan's head from the rest of him. The following day I managed to take one more ptarmigan out on the open tundra that I caught running through some low-lying brush.

The single shot 16 gauge, and the headless ptarmigan.

As the week came to an end, I realized that the northland had cast its magical spell upon me once again. I had experienced such a great time sharing this hunt with my dad, and had made several new friends. The northern lights had provided us with breathtaking nightly displays, and Brian and Cindy's hard work ethic, generosity, and uncommon kindness had once again added so much more to an already great hunt. Earlier in the week I had told Brian and Cindy that I thought the name of the camp should be changed from Coursoulles to cold souls, but from out of the cold, came some unexpected warmth for my soul. I'm the type of person that likes to name inanimate objects that have a significant meaning to me, so I thought maybe the name would fit my beloved 30/06 a little better, it would serve as a reminder of an unbelievable hunt shared with my father, and after all if anything has a cold soul it's my hunting rifle.

The monster I saw on the second to the last day of the hunt when all caribou tags had already been filled. This caribou is what dreams are made of, and he still haunts me. This caribou had it all. You can't really see it but he has a double shovel which is very deep, also tall tops, extremely palmated bez with lots of points, and a wide spread.

BE YOUR OWN HERO

Growing up, like most kids, I was searching for someone to look up to. Someone who had life's answers, and could tell me how to be successful. As a teenager, I lived in northern Maine for a year. There I met an excellent role model. He was a magnificent deer hunter. In a land where deer are scarce in general, he not only killed deer every year, but he consistently killed giant 200 plus pound bucks. He is a successful business man who runs his own guide service. He had the fortitude to build, by hand, start to finish, several small cabins for his clients, as well as a beautiful log home for himself and his family. He hand peeled the logs and the whole bit. Since my teenage years, he has become a well-known legend amongst deer hunters.

He taught me many lessons, one of which was not to place so much stock in a role model, because they will eventually let you down as he did me, not that I hold it against him. Even great people are human. Don't put your faith in me because I will eventually let you down too. You need to look up to yourself not others. It took me a while, but I finally learned that the only person to put my faith in who would not let me down, is me. You won't find the answers to life's questions through somebody else, but they will come from within. Don't let yourself down, because everyone else eventually will. The people who constantly let themselves down by being quitters, and taking the easy route by giving up, are often the sad, depressed, and confused people in life who often can't figure out why they are the way they are. It's easy to quit, but keep persevering no matter how impossibly huge the obstacle in front of you is. Pursue it with steady and constant dogged determination. No matter how many times you get kicked down, keep coming back, and you will be amazed by what you eventually can accomplish. If you fail, well that hurts pretty badly, but at least you can sleep at night. If you quit, there's a little piece of you inside, whether you realize it at the time or not, that is ashamed and disgusted with yourself. If you do it enough, you eventually won't like, and even won't be able to live with yourself.

The deer slayer from Maine told me once while we were fly fishing for trout that he didn't care how hard he had to work as long as he got what he wanted in the end. A principal that he obviously has lived by, and a motto that I've adopted myself — it has served me well. I've learned that the secrets to success are persistence, perseverance, fierce drive, and fierce determination. Spend time in the woods hunting, trapping, and fishing, and mother nature will eventually teach you these lessons along with a good dose of common sense. My whole life people have underestimated me, and doubted my abilities in the endeavors that I have taken on. I've made a game out of proving them wrong. Hold the people that trusted you, and demonstrated that trust before you had proven yourself in a place of honor. Other "friends," and even family, will come out of the woodwork after you are successful. Once you're "accomplished" suddenly they love and adore you. Don't be fooled, hold these people at arms length, they are the same ones who, as soon as you fall, step on your neck while they attain a better vantage point from which to steal what you have accomplished. As soon as your not doing well anymore, then you will be useless to them once again. With perseverance, persistence, fierce drive, furious determination, common sense, trust in Christ, and a handful of other good qualities learned in the outdoor classroom, you will go much further than most "intelligent" college graduates. Some people might say this is a "cynical" or "hard" view, but the reality is that it's a hard world, and your going to have to have a hard side to be successful in dealing with it. The secret is to have a soft side as well, and to make sure to try and not bring the hard side home with you at the end of the day.

Another thing that I think is important, as far as being successful is concerned, is not to get wrapped up in drugs or alcohol. I don't use them in any capacity and would recommend that you don't either. They will rob you of your drive and determination. They will make you weak minded, and eventually weak in the body as well.

These are the answers, and secrets to success in everything from deer hunting to business. These are the secrets that I was looking for as a young man, and wished somebody had told me. They are not a quick fix or miracle answers, but lots of hard work. They have taken me far, and will you as well.

8

HUNT ALONE OR WITH FRIENDS?

I'd like to talk about some of the advantages, and disadvantages of hunting with others or alone. I think the vast majority of people are inclined to hunt in a group. There are a lot of advantages to hunting with a few other hunters, but there are also some very alluring aspects to the solo hunt. I'd say that I hunted alone 90 percent of the time until I reached the age of about 28. The small amount of time spent hunting with other hunters would mostly have been with my dad, or the rare occasion when I'd go out with a friend. The last few years I've found several other hunters that I really enjoy hunting with, and I'd say that I hunt with them about half of the time. The camaraderie is a big draw to hunting with other hunters, and man seems to derive more satisfaction when he has someone to share his successes with.

THE SOLO HUNTER

One of the advantages to hunting alone is you have no pre-set schedule. You're free to travel as far as you'd like, and to hunt wherever your hunter's instincts draw you. There have been, times when hunting in a group, we had split up, and agreed to meet back at the truck at a certain time. Occasionally, it feels as though your just getting into a good hunting area, and you have to leave it behind to get back to the truck because of the time constraint. Your hunter's instincts may be drawing you in a certain direction, but if you've agreed to walk a predetermined route with your hunting buddies, it's only right to stick to what your hunting partners are relying on you to do. Ultimately, you have more freedom when you hunt alone. There is nobody else to influence how you hunt, where you hunt, or what time you have to stop hunting. Plus, there is nobody to help by kicking a deer out to you; you truly have to match your skills to that of your quarry.

E.A. Russell with the results of a solo hunt. He calls this one the "doe in heat buck." All he saw was the ear and antler. He promptly shot under the antler and you can see the results.

The solo hunter is a true hunter, and thoroughly loves the hunt and is in tune with the wilderness. He doesn't have to travel to far away lands, but is happy just to find, and seek out adventure in the local deer woods. He doesn't need anyone to prompt him to take to the woods, but desires the experience so much that he's willing to go by himself. He leaves his bed while it's still dark and enters the cold woods under the same darkness without any prompting, and knowing full well the odds are against him. Over the years he's learned that hard nose persistence will eventually pay off. First light finds him on the backside of some lonely ridge working the edge of a swamp despite the cold, dark, overcast day, and rain that would dampen many hunters' spirits. It's a lonely place of solitude, and as he actually becomes a part of the wet landscape, his predator eyes constantly scan for his quarry. This is a man that loves the hunt; the comforts of a warm easy chair have undoubtedly lured many a lesser hunter away from the woods on a day like this.

> *"I am often asked if I am not lonely on my solitary excursions. It seems so self-evident that one cannot be lonesome where everything is wild and beautiful and busy and steeped with God that the question is hard to answer."*
>
> ~ *John Muir*

GROUP HUNTING

Unlike the solo hunter, hunters hunting in a group don't necessarily have to be serious hunters, although oftentimes they are. Sometimes, one is there because that's what their buddies are doing that weekend, though it's not something that person would go out and do on their own. When a deer is pushed by a hunter, it is immediately more vulnerable because it is moving. It has less time to sort out smells, and detect danger, and will often walk blindly into the crosshairs of a waiting hunter. When you have a deer up and moving between hunters, a greenhorn has as much chance of seeing that animal as does the man with the most hunting seasons under his belt. In that respect, this is a great way for a new hunter to have immediate success in the deer woods. There should be at least a few experienced hunters in the group that recognize pinch points, and other features in the terrain that should be exploited.

The results of hunting in a group can be very rewarding when the hunters know each other, and the land. These three deer were on the ground by nine in the morning. These three does were taken in New Hampshire's unit M on the doe only tag available there. Pictured are Fran Perreault, Joe Perreault, and the author holding his side lock muzzleloader.

Hunting with a few other hunters can be very rewarding both in the camaraderie aspect as well as in success in killing deer. If a group of hunters know the terrain, and the travel routes of the deer, and especially, if they know each other well, they can combine their efforts, and work in unison to flush out animals for each other, and ultimately be more successful than the lone hunter.

Once again the results of group hunting are plain to see. These animals were taken within the first hour of opening morning along the Saco River in Maine. Pictured are Craig Aderman and son Daniel, and also Gerald Keismond.

You also learn a great deal when you hunt with others, especially those who have more experience than yourself. Further on in this chapter you will get to hear from some other hunters, and hear some of the advice that has made them successful. Like I said, there is a great deal to be learned through hunting with others, and hopefully you will pick something up from them.

David Haine is a local realtor whom I got to know on a caribou hunt in Newfoundland. David is not featured in this section, but as you get to know him later in the book, he will give plenty of advice concerning bog hunting, and finding wild edible mushrooms. I can remember a hunt when I first started hunting with David. David was hunting off to my left, and I had two deer approach from my right. I killed one of the deer as soon as my crosshairs settled on its shoulder, and the other deer ran back to the right where it had come from. When David realized the scenario, he asked why I had not let the deer get by me before taking one — then the second one likely would have run in David's general direction. It seemed like such basic common sense that I felt a bit selfish, and even, a touch ashamed that I had not had the presence of mind to think of such a thing. I was used to hunting alone, and over time had trained myself to shoot as soon as a killing shot presented itself. This is a good example of a lesson learned through hunting with others.

A WORD OF CAUTION

Hunters hunting in a group are not always serious hunters, and there is nothing wrong with that. As long as they are safety conscious, there's nothing wrong with a recreational weekend spent in the woods. I am, however, careful of whom I hunt with, and often am leery of new hunting partners, and how their hunting style might mesh with mine. I am definitely not the type of person that likes to hunt in a large gang. I recall, one time in my early twenties, when I made plans to hunt with a local contractor whom I did not know very well, and several of his friends. I should have known at the outset what the day was to hold as they bragged about their hunting prowess, and all the deer they were going to kill. Generally the true woodsman is slightly more humble. They used me for a hound dog the entire day, and expected me to be in certain places at certain times. I don't mind walking, and I spent the entire day pushing miles of unfamiliar territory for these guys with my compass to help keep me on course. Considering that I was unfamiliar with the land where we were hunting, I occasionally came out at the wrong spot, or arrived later than I was supposed to, and their unappreciative attitude was very discouraging. I did not realize how much walking I was going to be doing that day and did not pack enough water. By the days end, I couldn't walk ten yards without getting severe cramps in my legs. None of these guys seemed to have hunted together much, and the effort was very loosely organized. This was the last time I hunted with this group. They did, however, teach me a very valuable lesson at a young age. I've learned to be very leery of new hunting groups, and generally to be careful of whom I hunt with. It definitely helps when hunting in a group if the pushes are well organized, and the territory can be much more effectively covered by someone who knows the lay of the land and where the deer are likely to be. Hunting time is far too valuable to settle for anything less.

HUNTERS I'VE KNOWN

While on the subject of hunting with other people, I think it would be a good time to talk about some of the hunters I've known. Over the years I've been lucky to share the hunt with a lot of knowledgeable hunters, and they have all had an influence on me in one way or another. These guys that I'm going to mention are not the casual hunter, or the guy that doesn't really care if he gets a deer or not. I feel these guys have taken hunting to another, more serious, level. All of these men are family men, and have or are bringing up families. It's no accident that they are successful in the woods. Most of them are successful business men, and without exception they are all hard workers. Once you've learned the qualities needed to be successful at one thing, they can be applied to any endeavor you choose. The outdoors will teach you these good qualities.

"In all things of nature there is something of the marvelous."
~Aristotle

Perseverance, persistence, patience, fierce drive and furious determination. I see these qualities in all the guys written about in this chapter. The three P's, in my opinion, are the most important and will take you far. You don't necessarily have to be smart, although it helps greatly. If you keep persevering, persisting, and have enough patience, you will eventually be successful. Even somebody with a college education is useless without at least a few of these good qualities. If they do not have the perseverance, or persistence to apply their college education, they will go no where, and all those "smarts" will have done them no good. We all know people who fit that bill. With that in mind, I'll move on to some of the hunters I've shared the woods with. I've asked each one of these hunters to share some advice with the reader. A piece of advice that has made them successful in the woods, and that may also benefit you.

Lou Gagnon with a real nice Maine buck.

LOU GAGNON

One guy that helped instill the love of the hunt while I was growing up is Lou Gagnon. He is what comes to mind when one conjures up the image of the classic God-fearing Yankee deer slayer. He has spent his lifetime in the Maine woods. The experience he has to draw on just from the sheer numbers of whitetails that have fallen to the report of his rifle is unrivaled by most. This man loves the woods, and I can assure you that any whitetail that is unfortunate enough to enter his line of vision will soon find itself neatly, and efficiently stacked away in somebody's freezer. Lou was taken under the wing of Norman Gray as a young man. Mr. Gray has since passed away, but still remains one of

64

Maine's most well known and respected trappers. Lou had the good fortune to spend several seasons as a full time trapper, and his knowledge of the natural world runs much deeper than just the whitetail deer. Anyone who knows him will tell you that Lou is a good man in the woods. We've shared hunting camps from Maine to as far away as the backwoods of northern Georgia where, along with my Dad, and a few others, we hunted out of a tent.

Lou's first big game kill took place when he was 12 years old. I think we can all remember how badly we wanted to get our first deer. Keep that in mind as I tell this story. Lou had shot a spike horn buck during the early part of the hunting season during his twelfth year. After he had made a killing shot, it ran to another hunter who finished it off, and then insisted on keeping it. Can you imagine the excitement of following up the blood trail of your first deer at 12 years old, and then the disappointment of losing the deer to another hunter? Well, the last day of the deer hunting season rolled around, and Lou waited for his dad to go to work, and then asked his mother if he could go hunting instead of to school. He knew his mother would let him go, and that his father would not. She did indeed let him hunt on the last day of the season. Lou climbed a mountain to his favorite hunting area. After spending the day in the woods, he finally admitted defeat, and started for home so as to be there before his father got there. He said he was following along an old logging road with his head hung low, as he was pretty disappointed about the season being over and not getting his deer. As he plodded along, he heard a low grunting noise almost like a pig would make, and he snapped his head up to see a black bear standing in front of him. He shot the bear, it ran off, and he ran all the way home to get help. They did indeed find the expired bear. Lou's mom sent the hide off to Pennsylvania to be tanned, and he still has it to this day. That's an incredible success for such a young hunter hunting alone, and that's how this Maine woodsman got his start.

Lou's advice has to do with animal behavior. You may wonder what knowing a fox or coyote so thoroughly that you can make them step on a two-inch trap pan submerged beneath the dirt has to do with deer hunting. All of the animals interact with each other as well as the land, and the better you understand the entire picture, the better you will become as an outdoorsman and wild game hunter. When Lou steps into the woods, every sight, sound, and smell, to which the casual observer may not take notice, has a meaning. It might be the cry of a blue jay, or a few nipped buds from the shoot of a small tree that makes him take notice, but being a trapper lends to a deeper level of meaning and understanding. His advice to you is printed below, and if I were you I'd pay attention, I know I hung on to every word.

Learn your Animal by Lou Gagnon

Lou Gagnon poses with a coyote in a foothold trap. Show me a man that regularly takes coyotes, and bears, and I'll show you a talented woodsman.

My trapping mentor, Norm Gray, didn't just teach me how to set traps to catch animals. He was always teaching me about why an animal was in a certain spot at a certain time. Animals don't live the haphazard life many think they do. They do things and go places for very specific reasons. The one possible exception is when they are spooked, and even then they, can be very predictable as to where they will look for safety.

Why do foxes always visit the highest point of land in a field? Why are the biggest boar coons in the hardwoods in late November? If I see an otter today, how long will it take him to come back? Why do the biggest bears only hit my bait once a week? Why do deer stop coming to fields in early to mid October? Where did all the bucks go that I saw in preseason? If I'm going to get an animal to step on a two- to four-inch trap pan, or go through a certain opening, I'd better know where he is and why he's there. I can't shoot big game if I don't see it. I won't see it consistently if I don't know where it is, and why it's there.

Lou Gagnon poses with a few furs that he trapped.

Another beautiful Maine buck meets it's demise compliments of Lou Gagnon.

An animal's behavior centers around **getting food, feeling safe, and breeding**, not necessarily in that order. Simply put, if you want consistent success, learn your animal. Each species has characteristics that are unique and predictable to that species, but don't forget to factor in that each animal of a species is also an individual, and this is what keeps things interesting, as well as challenging. Once you've learned your animal, you can take that knowledge anywhere, and simply by looking at a topographical map you can form a plan you feel good about. Knowledge leads to confidence, and confidence leads to success.

That's the end of what Lou had written. He was going to leave you guessing about the coon in the hardwoods, the fox always attaining the summit of the land in a field, etc. I'd like to say that I knew all the answers to the questions he asked myself, but that coon in the hardwoods stumped me as did a few others. I had to call Lou back and these are the explanations he gave.

The large male raccoons stay out later in the season to try and fatten up more for hibernation. Once the lowlands begin to freeze in the middle part of November the females will go to den. They are no longer able to get crayfish and other aquatic foods that are the staples of their diet. The big boars will stay out later and move onto the hardwood ridges to really fatten up on the beechnuts, acorns, and what not. Lou says he's gotten some of his largest coons at this time of year and at the hardwood location. They are always big males, and never females.

Why does the fox always gravitate to the summit of land in a field? I loved Lou's explanation on this one: Why would the school geek try and attain a vantage point from which to survey the schoolyard before entering it? Because he's used to getting his ass kicked by the school bully. Being used to getting his ass kicked makes him a cautious sort of an animal. Basically the fox knows if there are any coyote's about he's going to get chased down, and get the snot beat out of himself.

Otters run a circuit made up of interconnecting waterways, rivers, streams, ponds, and bogs. They eventually will return to where you had seen them. Lone males and adults will probably run a bigger circuit, and may not return for a month or more, but females with young may be back in two to three weeks. Lou mentions that generally the males of any species usually have a larger territory than the females of the same species. The good news is every otter in the area will likely visit the spot that you saw the otter, or if you've found an otter toilet sight, so set a trap any way.

The big bears only visit the bait sight once a week for the same reason. They have a larger territory that brings them back less frequently. They are cagey ol boys that just aren't going to hang around a bait sight like the smaller bears will. The good news, says Lou, is that once you figure there pattern, they can be predictable.

Why do deer stop frequenting the fields in mid October? Deer stop frequenting the fields in mid October because some of the nuts are starting to fall. It's a change in diet that basically changes their habits. Lou says the change can be especially noticeable and abrupt if you get some windy weather around the middle of the month. What's happening is, as the wind blows, the branches start to drop some of the nuts. So, if you're a bow hunter, and see an abrupt change in deer sign (a lack of sign under your stand or in your area), look to the nearest hardwood ridge, and there is a good chance you'll be back in the action.

The last answer is to the question Lou asked about why the bucks you were seeing in the pre-season disappear. They start to get out of their summer pattern of food and safety, which also might dictate them staying in a smaller area where you have been seeing them. With the changing of the season, breeding starts to enter the thoughts of these big bucks. They start to expand their territories and start looking for does and areas that contain lots of does. This is also the time of year when they start to feel a little bit of pressure from hunters, therefore, it doesn't take much to make them completely nocturnal.

In the part of this chapter that Lou actually wrote, he mentioned that **"an animal's behavior centers around getting food, feeling safe and breeding."** The fox's behavior in the field centers around **"feeling safe,"** and so does the buck's when he goes nocturnal. The deer's behavior changes as the nuts begin to fall in mid-October which would take care of the "getting food" part, and the raccoon in the hardwoods is also predictable due to **the "getting food"** part. The buck disappears, or changes his behavior as a result of the **"breeding"** urge. Well, that pretty well sums it up. I'd say Lou covered his bases pretty well wouldn't you? Take Lou's advice — **learn your animal.**

I called Lou on the phone to get his answers to the questions he asked in his writing. When he was done giving me the answers, he queried if that made me as good a woodsman as him now? No, not quite yet, Lou, but you better watch your back track ol boy, I'm gonna catch you one of these years!

Bill Frasier and just a few of the many great racks he's taken over the years.

BILL FRASIER

Bill Frasier has killed at least one deer consecutively for over 30 years running. Quite an accomplishment considering there have been some hard winters, and big deer losses in that time. He's a great hunter, and I've had the privilege to hunt with him on occasion.

Bill has taken many great bucks, and his fair share of 200 pounders. Bill has an attention to detail that most don't share. Simply put, things have to be right. I like that about him, and that's what I attribute to his many successes in the outdoors. At one point in his life he was a competitive shooter and, along with his shooting partners, won many contests. Bill has shot the majority of his deer either in the head or the neck. At one point the people checking his deer remarked that they had never seen so many head-shot deer. I don't recommend this shot except for the most skilled shooter, and the man with nerves of steel under pressure. Believe me when I tell you Bill is this guy. Most people, myself included, are much better off aiming for the "boiler room." For those of you who do not know, the boiler room is the chest cavity which contains the heart and lungs. The best way to locate this area is to aim at, or just behind the shoulder, depending on how the deer is standing or quartering. This is the shot that is widely accepted as the best aiming point for deer, with a double lung shot being the "ideal shot."

Before anybody starts getting nervous about whether they think a head shot is a high percentage shot, let me say that in that 30-year streak, Bill has never missed a deer, and has only wounded one that he could not find, and all I'll say about that is that the head neck area was not the aiming point. He generally does not shoot at running deer, and waits for the right shot. In my way of thinking this is an awesome display of patience. I can't say it often enough — patience is a very important aspect of being a successful hunter and Bill has a quiet, confident kind of patience that you can sense about him. This is a man that's going to get what he's after, it's just a matter of time. Below is Bill's advice to the reader just the way he wrote it. It's some of my favorite advice. I liked it enough that I wrote it exactly as he did. Like the man it's quick, concise, to the point, and good. He's killed some wicked bucks following the advice printed below. You will also get a sense of Bill's deep admiration for the coyote.

The Most Important Tip I Could Give a Fellow Hunter

Hunt the same area as much as you possibly can! Learn as much as you can about this particular piece of woods! Where do you always see fresh signs (tracks, rubs, scrapes or browsing)? Where do you always see the most signs? Where do you usually see or jump deer on this property? Where have you seen deer on real cold days, warm days, rainy days, snowy days or very windy days? Learn about the predominant wind direction on this property. Learn where the heaviest concentration of oak and beech trees are located. If we are going out to pick blueberries or fiddleheads, we want to go to an area of high concentration. Deer can be just as lazy as people! Pay particular attention to where deer cross brooks and streams on this piece of property. Deer tend to cross in the same spots all the time. When you see a well-worn game trail while you are hunting or scouting, think how many years of use this same trail has gotten. Try to observe the pinch points and the funnel areas that all deer are likely to travel through. Always be looking for a good tree to hang a stand in. Like in the old days we were always looking for a good Christmas tree to come back and harvest in December.

From your above observations and knowledge of the area, you should be able to put together a game plan for hunting this area. Each day may require a slight change of plans, such as wind direction or weather on that particular day. Try to spend most of your day hunting in the hot spots you've discovered. If you hunt very carefully in these areas and more rapidly in the woods between your hot spots, you will be more successful.

Always remember to put something new in the memory bank every day you hunt, and don't be afraid to shoot a coyote. Good luck.

Bill Frasier 1-13-09

JOE PERREAULT

Another hunter I'd like to mention, and somebody I've started hunting with in recent years, is Joe Perreault. He lives in the southern part of New Hampshire with his wife Lisa and two kids Bryce, and Mya. Joey, like myself, is a family man, and it's evident what the most important aspect of his life is. It sounds cliché, but the first time I hunted with Joe was like slipping on an old pair of hunting boots. It just felt right. It seemed as if we'd been hunting together for years. There was no awkwardness in hunting style; it just clicked. Joey knows his hunting areas, and how to hunt them. He has several nice bucks to his credit, and many deer with a bow under his belt, which in my book is a great accomplishment.

Joey Perreault and a beautiful New Hampshire nine point taken with a muzzleloader. Only the muzzleloaders cap went off with the first shot. Fortunately the buck waited for Joe to put another cap on, and shoot again. This buck was the result of a well placed tree stand.

The very first time I hunted with Joe I killed a doe, due mostly in part to Joey's knowledge of his hunting area. The hunt was all but over, we were on our way out to the trucks, and maybe only 10 minutes away. I was hunting with a muzzleloader, and we were pushing out through a ravine. We had a guy on the right side of the ravine, a guy walking in the thick stuff at the bottom, and me on the left-hand side of the ravine. I heard the guy in the bottom yell, and sure enough out pops a couple of does running on the edge of the thick stuff at the bottom of the ravine. When they decided to cut up the steep hillside in front of me into the open hardwoods, things got serious. I followed the lead deer bounding trying to catch her in openings with my scope. The whole thing happened pretty quickly, but when I glimpsed my crosshairs on her shoulder I touched my muzzleloader off. The results were instantaneous, and spectacular. When the smoke cleared she had collapsed from mid air, and started sliding back down the steep hillside. It's an image that's burned into my memory — one I'll never forget. To date it's the best running shot I've ever made. At about 45 yards with a muzzleloader I broke her spine. I'm sure a bit of luck was involved, but I'd also like to think the thousands of rounds I've burnt at the range didn't hurt either. Joe was able to set up a buddy stand and get his son Bryce a shot at a spike horn the very same year. At the age of eight, he capitalized on it. That's a commitment to passing on to the next generation. What an accomplishment, for both father and son, for the boy to take down his first deer at age eight. I consider Joe a true friend, and in short Joe is good people.

Joe's son Bryce Perreault with a nice looking spike horn taken with a 12 gauge shotgun at age eight. Looks like a proud hunter, and rightfully so.

Be Prepared Mentally

Joey's advice to his fellow hunter is to be prepared mentally. He says that it all starts at the shooting range, and I couldn't agree more. He has a mental checklist that he goes through when he sees an animal that he is going to take. This mental checklist helps him through the process of taking the animal, and minimizes buck fever. If he's constantly telling himself to look for an opening, look for the shoulder, and look for a spot while avoiding being distracted by the antlers or making other mistakes, he isn't apt to get buck fever. In other words he keeps his mind occupied with a list of things that ultimately lead to a well-placed shot. Joey, like many other experienced hunters will tell you that the wind is not just important, it makes or breaks the deal. Another thing that I have observed about Joe is that he knows every inch of his hunting areas, and he knows how to hunt them. He's hunted the same areas for years, and he knows where the deer will likely go.

ELBRIDGE RUSSELL

One hunter who has set himself apart from the crowd is Elbridge Russell. With a name like Elbridge he was going to be either really good or badly. I'm happy to say that he came out on the good side of things. He's a tall slender man with pale blue eyes. The last thing I'd want to see is those eyes peering at me over the barrel of a gun. He says he's shooting all those big bucks, but he might just be scarin' 'em to death. All joking aside, the Russell boys put some deer on the pole, and some nice bucks thrown in for good measure.

WOW! You know that good deeya came from Maine! E.A. Russell with the monster he calls the "king of the mountain."

75

Elbridge standing at the end of his log cabin. He keeps the big ones inside.

Elbridge is the local Maine boy that done right. He started out as a young man shooting his first buck, a 172-pound six-point, at age 14, and he was hooked. After finishing school, he became a Navy pilot and learned "attention to detail." Upon discharge he returned home to run a canoe business and his small sawmill and now he owns hundreds of acres that he manages for timber.

Elbridge has killed what I would consider an impressive amount of bucks and some true giants. He's as good as any hunter that I know, and when Elbridge talks deer hunting, I'm all ears. The buck he calls the King of the mountain was taken on a lousy, rainy day as he still hunted a ridge top. He saw the top two inches of antler and could see a piece of the deer's shoulder through a small opening in a beech tree which he promptly fired at. The buck turned out to be six and a half years old with a huge rack for a Maine deer. Elbridge sends in a tooth to a biologist to age his bucks. The oldest buck he's taken was nine-and one-half years old. The biologist said that it was 1 in 10,000 for a wild Maine deer to reach such an old age. In a land where many good hunters never get a decent buck over the course of their lifetime, Elbridge has managed to rack up an impressive display of bucks.

I think that it is also worth noting that Elbridge has some of the most interesting deer stands I have ever seen. He has one that he calls the "Inside the tree stand." It consists of a gigantic maple that several men couldn't stand hand-in-hand and reach around. About seven feet up, the tree branches grow off into several gigantic leaders leaving a hollow spot in the middle. Elbridge hung some burlap to act as a blind, and has a wooden ladder leading up to the hollow spot in the tree. It's a very comfortable stand to hunt out of, and, to top it off several well-used deer trails converged within spitting distance of the tree on the day he showed it to me. He has another stand that is nestled into the side of a cliff. Yet another stand consists of a gigantic hollow tree butt that you actually stand inside. The tree is broken off at just the right level so that nothing but your head pokes out.

Dick Marshall pictured in the "inside the tree stand"

The last stand that I will describe was built for his son. It's a tree that had fallen over and landed in the crotch of another upright tree, probably 12 to 15 feet off the ground. The tree that fell over is still rooted in the ground and still alive. It acts as a ramp to walk up to the hunting platform near the crotch that

Elbridge built complete with railings, and five gallon buckets to sit on. He drove 12-inch spikes the length of the "ramp" to give a hand-and-foot hold as you climb. The whole thing leans and each tree acts as an anchor for the other. Without the support of the ramp tree, the other would fall over sideways, and obviously the ramp tree is supported by the upright tree's crotch. Obviously, the stand is located in an excellent spot for seeing deer.

Jimmy Russell with his first deer, and a nice buck at that. Pictured with uncle Larry Kiesman, "the master"

As we sat in the "ramp stand" Elbridge shared a hunt with me that had taken place with his son in that very stand. His son had shot at and missed a small buck. The buck not knowing where the shot had come from actually ran over and stood directly under the stand. His son already had buck fever, and looking down at that deer through the cracks in the platform boards of the tree stand really got him riled up. After shooting at, and missing several easy shots, he finally hit it with his last bullet on a far away difficult shot. You could sense the excitement in Elbridge's voice as he relived the story. It goes without saying that it was a very exciting hunt for both father and son. Elbridge has succeeded in passing the torch on to the next generation.

E.A. Russell with the eight point the calls the foggy morning "flower garden buck." The flower garden is a 300 acre swamp that got it's name because orchids sprout up out of it, but only on drought years.

Now that we know a little about Elbridge, and his background I'll go ahead, and tell you that Elbridge's advice has to do with still hunting. However, before we get to his advice, I would like to share a story that ties in with the subject. I hunted with a Marine who was in his mid twenties one year. He had just gotten back from Iraq where he had been involved in some of the fiercest fighting of the war. He had killed men, and been shot at himself, and the fighting was so fierce that he had gone days at a time without sleep. I thought I hunted slow, but when he entered the woods, he was in a crouched position with his senses on full alert as he constantly scanned with his eyes. He had his firearm at the ready just below his shoulder. He was hunting at a snail's pace, and moving through the woods as though his life depended on it, as if somebody was going to jump out and shoot back. He used every bit of concealment to his advantage, again, as though his life depended on it. I have to tell you that it was quite an inspiration to watch.

It's important to note that while still hunting, you want to truly slow down and take your time, especially where the deer sign warrants it. I remember a hunt with Joe Perreault when we hunted a piece of woods that we had not hunted that season. There was snow on the ground, and over the course of traversing the entire wood lot, all we saw was a doe and a skipper track that was several days old on week-old snow. If we had spent hours meticulously hunting, and picking apart the woods, it wouldn't have made much sense. You want to take meticulous care where you know from past experience there are deer, or when in a new piece of woods you start to see very fresh sign.

Jim Whytock with the "Octagon eight point."
This buck came in to a scent bomb with his nose in the air.
Jim is a member of Elbridge Russell's hunting group.

I would encourage you to study what Elbridge has written, and to truly act out his advice. It's easy to get discouraged and dismiss what has been written and go back to hunting how you normally would. It requires much patience, which is one of the three "Ps" that I talked about earlier. I believe that if you can master his advice, you will have taken your still hunting game to another level. One last thought before we get to the advice — Dick Proenneke said **"to see game you must move a little, and look a lot."** With that in mind I will go ahead and list Elbridge's advice as it concerns to still hunting.

**Another "flower garden buck" taken by E.A. Russell,
this one a 196 pound nine point.**

STILL HUNTING ADVICE

MY KEYS TO STILL HUNTING by Elbridge Russell

1. Work at keeping your clothes clean and scent free.

2. Try not to walk more than five steps and then stop, hopefully next to something (not only for concealment, but also for a shooting rest if you're lucky). Certainly never take more than ten steps.

3. Don't walk fast! Walk slow enough to spend more than 60 percent of your time scanning for game or parts of game. Use your eyes to look ahead, and not at the deer sign or tracks on the ground. I knew a hunter once who never had

a lot of luck in the deer woods. He sustained an injury to one of his legs that slowed him down considerably. It's unfortunate that he was injured, but wouldn't you know it, he started consistently killing deer afterwards.

4. Move in the darker, thicker growth. Be "inside" looking out, like the buck, and then stop, look and listen.

5. When you find the "right spot," wait to move for 10 minutes, or sit down for 30-plus minutes before moving on.

6. Try to keep track of where the wind is blowing, and always try to keep it off your back.

7. Get in the woods, and stay in the woods as often as possible. By stay in the woods, I mean don't go to the local diner at lunch time, but pack your lunch. Hunt all day if you can.

CHARLES MATTOCKS

An outdoorsman with whom I spent countless hours hunting and fishing is Charles Mattocks, better known as "Chick." I met Chick about the time I graduated high school, and a few years after he had retired. I wasn't yet serious about working, and he was done working, and ready to play again. So there was a couple of years when we were pretty much inseparable, and to say we hunted and fished a lot would be an understatement. We shared hunting camps together as far away as Maryland and New York.

We fished the ocean and as far north as the tip of Maine. He was the only person I knew at the time who liked to hunt and fish as much as I did. He didn't tire, and start thinking of home halfway through the day, but wanted to stay out the whole day as did I. He instilled in me his knowledge and love for ice fishing for lake trout, and trolling for salmon at ice-out in the spring. Lake Winnipesaukee was one of our most notorious haunts for both ice fishing and salmon fishing. Chick had a large influence on me at a time when I was learning, and honing my outdoor skills. He was a very meticulous man —

things had to be right. He was a reloader, and had spent time as a sheet metal worker where he worked within thousands of an inch, which is what I correlate to him being so meticulous. He was also a callous man. He had been through a lot in his life. In his early 50s, he was diagnosed with cancer, and given a very small chance of survival. He gave away most of his firearms, and stuff that was near and dear to him as he thought he was going to die. After he had a lung removed he got better, and never had a recurrence. Chick was known to win rifle, and muzzleloader shooting competitions, as well as the running deer shoot at the local Fish and Game club. He reloaded for me, and coached me on my shooting. I know it was rewarding for him to watch me evolve from a mediocre rifle shot into a skilled shooter. Under his meticulous, and hard watch I gained mastery over not just the rifle, but pistol, muzzleloader as well as wing shooting. It's worthwhile to note that his lifelong wife Delia was as decent a Christian woman as I've ever known. She was practically a saint. She seemed to desire nothing materialistic, and if given a piece of jewelry by Chick would soon give it to one of her granddaughters. I have no doubt that they share a piece of heaven together.

Chick and myself after a successful goose hunt.

The last hunter I will talk about is my uncle Lewis Fernald. I feel he's reached legendary status due to the unique circumstances surrounding his life, and his incredible hunting track record, so I've devoted a chapter to him. Even though he's passed on, his chapter still comes complete with the hunting advice as he had given me some before he died.

9

LEWIS FERNALD: A NORTH WOODS LEGEND

Was Lewis Fernald the greatest bear slayer to ever roam the north woods of New England? I think he might just well have been. A statement like that probably raises a lot of eyebrows. However, so spectacular were his achievements that somebody is undoubtedly going to say it ain't true, it's not possible for one man acting alone to kill all those bears without the use of bait or hounds. I can assure you it's true. I've never even heard rumored of another man even coming close to racking up the numbers of bears that uncle Lewis did. I'm not saying that such a man doesn't or hasn't existed, I'm just saying I haven't heard of him. If Lewis wasn't the greatest bear slayer to roam the New England woods, he sure as heck ranks right up there near the top. I suppose there is a hound hunter somewhere in New England that may have come close, but it's important to note that uncle Lewis matched his skills to that of the bears without the aid of bait or hounds. Further more, the fact that he had a score to settle, or a vendetta if you will, and the unique circumstances surrounding it, are, in my mind, what propels him into legendary status. He had plenty of motivation to kill all those bears. Read on.

Lewis grew up in the Mountains of Jackson New Hampshire. It's a quaint little town that has developed into somewhat of a tourist trap. You cross a picture-perfect, single-lane, wooden-covered bridge to get into town, but the country is mountainous and rugged. Wealthy tourist sit inside there warm cozy vacation homes, and look out at the beauty. You might say they've inherited the land and all of its beauty without feeling the hardships that mountain living and harsh winters dish out. They've only cheated themselves, though. It's these types of hardships, that build character and a deeper sense of satisfaction and closeness to the land, that others can't fully understand or appreciate. This is not to take anything away from the wealthy tourist — I'm sure they've paid plenty of dues — just of a different kind. Far too often though they look out at those mountains from their cozy warmth without giving a second thought to the men and women, who lived in these hills, and knew the mountains and wilderness so well that they actually became a part of the land. When you lay on your belly and suck water straight from the veins of the mountain far from any hiking trail, and the lifeblood of the animals that derive nutrients from the mountainsides has provided you sustenance, you become part of the land. This is the story of just such a man. He lived out his life in the type of country where mountains grow sideways out of other mountains. You might say the land is beautiful but hard. This is the story of a man who plied these mountains. I went to visit Lewis's wife Roberta during the first week of January 2009 to get the details for this story, as Lewis himself has passed. I pulled into the driveway of a property cut into the side of a mountain where Lewis lived for so many years. Roberta started the story out when Lewis was seven years old, and here is my interpretation of how she told it.

When Lewis was seven years old, he lived with his family on their farm up on Black Mountain in Jackson, New Hampshire. His dad Arthur was having trouble with the bears killing his sheep, as were some of the other farmers living near by. The bears were so plentiful and problematic at the time that there was a bounty out on them. Once a bear started killing sheep the bear had to be killed as they would return relentlessly night after night once they had a taste for it. So Arthur set a trap for the problem bear up behind the farm in the woods. It was one of those big old leg-hold bear traps with a drag attached to it. The idea is that if the bear is attached to something solid he has something solid to pull against, and may pull his leg out as they are very powerful animals. If the bear is attached to a drag of some sorts, he can be tracked to a point where he is generally found with the drag entangled in the brush, which many times will have some give to it so the bear can't get a solid pull against the trap.

The year was 1927 and it was an early November morning when Arthur set out with his gun to check the bear trap. The mountain was about to unleash a fury as dark, and sinister as its name. Arthur did indeed find a bear in the trap, and he remembered a local photographer by the name of Pope, who wanted a picture of a live bear. Instead of dispatching the bear, he decided to go and get the photographer. The bear apparently was not tangled in the brush as tightly as he had thought because as soon as he turned his back to head toward town he was knocked to the ground and viciously mauled by the bear. Arthur covered his head and neck as best he could with his hands, and stayed laying on his stomach so as to protect his insides. The bear eventually left, and when he did Arthur started hollering.

Now, to a seven-year-old kid a dad is a symbol of strength, a provider and protector. I have a little girl, and she just thinks I'm the strongest, toughest guy in the world, and the last thing I would want her to see is her daddy getting hurt or injured. You can imagine how little Lewis must have felt when he found his dad beaten down into a broken bloody mess. So vicious was the mauling that Arthur would spend months in the hospital recovering. When Lewis found his dad, Arthur said to his son, "Now, boy, go and get me a pint of heavy cream." They kept cows, and Lewis did as he was told. Neither Roberta nor myself really knew what the cream was for, but Arthur drank it, and Roberta said they knew how to take care of themselves back in those days. Lewis got the farmer from the next farm down who went by the name of Ken Davis to come and help get his dad out of the woods. Once Arthur was at the hospital, Arthur's brother, Pearly Fernald, and Ken Davis went and killed the bear. Roberta admitted that Lewis had a bit of a grudge against bears from that point forward. It must have been horribly traumatic to see your dad in that kind of a predicament at such a young age. Lewis had already begun to feel the sting of the hardness in the mountains that he would grow to love so much.

I try to think back about when I was a little boy, and I bet I would have wanted to kill every bear I could lay eyes on, and I want to tell you mister, that's just what Lewis did. I'm holding a newspaper clipping provided by Roberta as I write this story, and the opening line to the article starts off to say, "Some people might think Lewis Fernald has a grudge against bears." Later it goes on to say that "Fernald has killed more bears in these parts than any other hunter." That was reported in the Wednesday, November second, 1983 edition of *The North Conway Reporter.*

Roberta said that years ago, hunting bears in the spring was allowed as well as in the fall, and that the spring season was Lewis's favorite time to hunt them because their pelts were absolutely beautiful. I think Lewis had more reasons to kill bears than just having a grudge. He obviously loved to hunt, and besides he was good at it. Roberta said there were years when he would kill three bears or more. I asked her how many bears he had killed in his lifetime, and she said there was no way of telling for sure, but probably as many as he was years old. Lewis died when he was 80, and furthermore, Roberta considers this a conservative estimate. Roberta was a great hunter in her own right. She's killed deer in excess of 200 pounds.

She laughed as she recalled a time when she was hunting with Lewis on the side of a mountain, and they spotted a bear. She shot the bear, and it started to tumble down the hillside toward them swatting, and fighting the invisible attacker that had stung it so severely. Now this bear was starting to get pretty darn close, and Lewis scrambled up over the hillside so as to get out of the way. Roberta never budged, she held her ground, and kept pumping the lead into the bear with her 44 magnum rifle. After the shooting had stopped, and the bear lay dead, not far away from her I might add, Lewis looked at her and said, "well, I guess you're not afraid of bears." They hunted together a fair bit, and Lewis wasn't one to give out a lot of compliments. So one thing that stuck with Roberta, and seemed to mean a lot to her, is that Lewis once told her he'd rather hunt with her than most of the men he had hunted with.

Besides the bear hunting Lewis was also a great deer hunter, and a throwback to the hunters of old. The respect that he commands as a hunter is evident, and awe inspiring even long after his passing. Any of the old time hunters that knew him speak of him with great respect as to his capability's in the woods. Lewis's son-in-law, though not a real serious hunter, had accompanied him on the occasional hunt. What I have gathered through conversation with him was that Lewis was most definitely a still hunter. He said that he was always on the move, and on rare occasion would stop for a few minutes to look an area over.

Bill Frasier had the good fortune to hunt with Lewis a few times. When asked about uncle Lewis, Bill told me the same thing that everyone else who knew him said, and that was that he never knew Lewis not to get his bear. Also, Lewis was always the guy getting the big buck. He killed many deer over 200 pounds. In 1968, he killed the biggest deer in New Hampshire that year. It dressed out at 267.5 pounds. Bill says that Lewis was always chewing on spruce gum. I've tried it, and don't see the allure. The other thing that Bill was able to tell me was that Lewis may have been somehow related to the Beloits, because he used there method of hunting before they had popularized it, which is to track down a big buck on the snow until a dead deer is the result.

I was never fortunate enough to have hunted with uncle Lewis, but he's with me on the hunt in spirit. I saw him at a family reunion when I was a teenager. It was after he had retired his rifle, and a few years before he died. He seemed a quiet man, and reluctant to tell a hunting story despite his many successes in the woods. For those of you looking for bear hunting advice from a north woods legend, I'll pass on to you what he told me.

He said this to me in regards to bear hunting — "hunt into the wind on a beech ridge while the nuts are falling." As Lewis aged, he began to have trouble, as we all will, and would occasionally fall, and somebody would have to be called to help him up as Roberta was unable. The decision was made by the family to see him into a nursing home. Roberta smiled as she said that the very year he left for the nursing home a six-point buck appeared in a small opening across the yard. This isn't like N.Y. or someplace where deer appear in front yards all of the time. This is a small opening in the woods on the side of a mountain where deer are scarce. Some hunters hunt their entire lives in this region, and never get a decent buck. I couldn't believe my ears as Roberta was telling me this story. It's almost as if Lewis had been sprinkled with some lucky fairy dust from above. I find it amazing that a man of his age, and in his shape was able to retrieve his rifle, go out on to the front deck, line up his sights, and drill that deer, and a buck at that, before it could escape. His condition was such that he was unable to track the buck and retrieve it himself — help had to be called. The great spirit of the hunt had smiled down, and shown favor upon this great hunter one last time, and in so doing put a golden seal on this hunter's destiny for legendary status. I can think of no greater way for a north woods legend to end his hunting career. I'm sure uncle Lewis can still be found in the hinterlands of the great beyond stalking a beech ridge with his nose pointed into the wind.

10

THE BEARS

Bears are a very interesting animals, and I've been lucky enough to have had a few experiences with them. They are a secretive animal, and are not generally seen in the woods by the casual observer. There are several animals that I would say are not commonly seen — one of which is the coyote, although I've been fortunate enough to see a handful over the years while deer hunting. The fisher, which is the larger cousin of the pine marten, is another animal that I've rarely seen in the woods other than in my traps. I was leaning up against a hemlock once while bow hunting, and the red squirrels around me started to go crazy, running up and down the trees, and chattering. A short time later, a fisher came bounding along in its nervous, high-strung kind of a lope, and just about ran over the tips of my feet. The fisher in no way reacted to me, and I don't believe he ever knew I was there as I sat motionless in my camo. In all the years spent in the woods, I've seen the fisher two other times while hunting. That being said, in all of the years spent deer hunting, scouting, etc., I've never *chanced* upon a bear. Hunting statistics in New England will confirm that this is not all that uncommon. The vast majority of bears taken in New Hampshire, and Maine are taken with the aid of bait or hounds. My experiences with bears have come while hunting them over bait. The small percentage of hunters that successfully take bears without the use of bait or hounds, generally luck upon them during deer hunting where the seasons overlap. The percentage of hunters that successfully target bear without the use of bait or hounds is even lower still. Out west, up in Alaska, or anywhere that the terrain is somewhat open, and the hunter can see across large distances would be the place for the bear hunter that wants to hunt without the use of hounds or bait. In open terrain, a bear can be spotted from a distance, and then the hunter can make adjustments for wind, and other factors to plan a successful stalk. This is not the case with the densely forested areas where New England bears reside.

**Lou Gagnon and a bear he trapped
with a leg snare.**

The bear's stomach is for sure his biggest weakness. This weakness gets him into all kinds of trouble. Old Mr. Bear finds trouble through his weakness not just with the hunter, but any where an easy meal might be found. He's known to cause excitement everywhere from birdfeeders to campgrounds, and of course it's always a huge bear causing the excitement. It's the nature of what I do as a wood carver to cater to the tourists, and I get to talk to a lot of out of state campers. It's fun to hear their bear stories, but what I have come to notice is that the stories always involve gigantic bears.

The unpopular truth is that the average New Hampshire bear is 150 pounds dressed weight. Do they get larger? Yes indeed, bears over 200 pounds abound, and even bears 300 pounds, and beyond, but they are the more rare exception as opposed to the rule. Ask any taxidermist who mounts his share of bears, and he will confirm this truth. Bears, in places like Pennsylvania, grow to larger sizes, up to 500 pounds or more, because they do not have the severe winters that we do. Shorter winters mean shorter hibernating times when bears don't eat, but instead live on fat stores. Bears are one of the hardest animals to judge as far as size is concerned, so I generally take issues of size with a grain of salt.

For a long time, I found it strange that the bears didn't seem to attack bird feeders immediately upon coming out of hibernation. You would think they would come out of their winter dens around the first of April, when the snow subsides, ravenous to eat whatever they could. It would seem that the first real rash of bear complaints comes more toward the end of may. If you think about it, the bear has had nothing to eat for several months while hibernating through the winter. I think he needs to eat something a little more delicate like grasses or something until he gets his appetite back. If you've been sick and you have had an empty stomach for a few days, when you start feeling better, you eat something gentle like soup until you get your appetite back. This is how I relate the delayed reaction time.

Some people don't feel as though baiting bear is an ethical way to hunt them. I obviously disagree, after all dead is dead. No matter the method you use to pursue bear, the ultimate goal is usually a dead bear. I think that the goal should be to dispatch the animal as humanely as possible, and that the method used to take the bear should be that which is most enjoyable to the hunter.

When a bear comes into a bait, he generally presents you with a close range standing-still shot, and on top of that a perfect shot angle. A still hunter might be shooting at a partially concealed or distant moving animal increasing the odds of wounding the bear. Another advantage to baiting is that you can avoid shooting sows with cubs as the cubs generally come in before the sow. In a normal hunting situation you might see the sow while her cub is concealed in the brush, and not find out what a horrible deed you've committed until after the shot. Hunting over bait is not as easy as some people may think. Some years the nuts, and berries are plentiful, and the bears are back in the mountains. They don't have to travel much to fill their bellies, so they are less likely to encounter a hunter's bait. Or with a full belly they may only come in after dark. Some years the nuts and berries are not so plentiful, and these are the best years to hunt. Hunting over bait is a hunt that is filled with excitement, and hopefully I convey that through my bear hunting stories.

Ultimately I don't think that we should knock the way that other people enjoy hunting. Just because we think our way may be more challenging or exciting doesn't mean we should beat other people's methods down to make ourselves feel more superior. The traditional archery crowd is notorious for this. I hunt with a recurve bow during bow season because this is what I enjoy, but I have no problem with the guy using a compound bow. I also love gun hunting, but to many of the die hard traditional archers all others are beneath them. Pick up a traditional archery publication, and you will immediately sense the cliquey snobbery, and superiority, and ultimately arrogance that I find so repulsive.

I had one traditional archer stop into my shop with his traditional bow who had obviously bought into this snobbery. He had the fanciest, most expensive equipment, and the bumper stickers confirming that he was a "serious" traditional archer. I have to admit that his bow looked like something out of a dream. The way he talked down about other hunters led me to believe he must have a ton of experience to back up that kind of arrogance. I was expecting to really possibly learn something from this man. I keep a target out behind my work area, and I was already starting to think of some questions for him concerning set up and tuning of the traditional bow. When we started shooting, my respect turned to suspicions as I realized he was nothing more than a buffoon with a big mouth and too much money. He was a chronic snap shooter, and could not hold his arrows in any kind of a group. His arrows flew not straight like a dart, but barrel rolled, and lurched wildly from side to side. When I began to ask him about some of these deficiencies, he became red faced, and defensive. I didn't push the issue, but instead let him continue to feel "superior." I couldn't help but feel bad for him as he waddled off to his truck with his fancy equipment in tow, his pants drooping as though he was carrying a load of unseen diarrhea. I knew that with his current attitude he was never going to improve.

Then there is the other end of the spectrum. There's another kind of arrogance when a man has achieved such a level of success in the woods as to be undeniable. I'm a little more tolerant of this because they've accomplished their goals through hard work, and hard-nose perseverance. On the same hand, I think they should try to avoid tearing down other hunters who simply are not as talented in the woods as they are, or who may have different methods of hunting.

A good example of this is some of the deer trackers who constantly kill big bucks. They may have a tendency to tear down the stand hunter. Some of these "lesser" hunters probably don't have the same experience, and confidence in their woodsmanship, and navigational skills to constantly track down and kill big bucks. This is not a weakness that should be preyed upon by the experienced hunter, but oftentimes this seems to be the case. Ultimately, all tearing down of others is done to try and make ourselves feel superior. Let accomplishments and actions speak for themselves.

Another method of bear hunting that I mentioned is hound hunting. I know very little of hound hunting other than the men that generally pursue this sport are usually serious woodsman. It's not a method of hunting that interests me to a great extent as I've obviously never pursued it. That's not to say that I wouldn't try it at some point in the future. It does sound somewhat exciting. Hounds men have some of the same advantages as the bait hunter in that they are afforded a close range shot, and can wait for a good shot angle. To hear them talk, they also find great pleasure in the music the hounds make as they take up the chase. I definitely think they should be allowed to pursue their sport.

That being said, there is a conflict that arises when dog hunting seasons are allowed to overlap bait hunting seasons. It used to be, in New Hampshire, that the bait hunters had the better part of September, and the hound hunters had October which I feel was perfectly fair. If the hound hunters want to go first, I have no problem with that either. I'd have no problem baiting during the month of October instead of September. The way the current rules have been set these past few years, the bait hunters are allowed only one week before the hound hunters are turned loose. This gives the hound hunters the better part of two months, and the baiters, a single week to themselves. One week is generally enough time to get a bear coming just in time for the hound hunters.

As a bait hunter, the first year this new rule took affect, I had a bad experience. I had anticipated the hunt for an entire year, I took time off from work to set up my sight, and run bait the first week. A lot of time, energy, preparation, juggling of schedules, and even money is put into this effort. I finally had a bear hit my sight and I made plans to hunt the following day. Imagine how my heart sank when I pulled into my area to hunt for the first time to find hound hunters, and hounds going everywhere. I found out through the grapevine that they killed three bears out of the area in the next week. I finished out the rest of the season with no more success at having a bear visit my sight. To top it off, bait hunters are only allowed two separate sights to hunt on, whereas the houndsmen can roam far and wide. I know it's not the hound hunters' fault, they were abiding by the law, but I think the law is flawed.

It seems to me that there is plenty of time for both parties to pursue there sport. I think its common sense to see that there is an obvious conflict. This begs the question of why our well-educated Fish and Game personnel have arranged such obviously flawed seasons even in the face of protest from the baiters? I know there has been protest because I've called and complained. There seems to be an obvious favoritism. Could it be that some of the wardens frequently use the hound hunters' dogs? Why not go back to giving each group a month? I have not baited bear for a few years out of frustration, but this year I applied for an area a mile from the nearest road, in a remote area. It will take more energy, time, and ultimately commitment to make the two-mile hike every day with a heavy load of bait going in, but I'm hoping that I will be out of the hound hunters' domain. What I do know is that I'll be better off for the exercise, and the experience in general.

Bear hunting over bait does take some mettle especially if the hunter is acting alone. There are a lot of "tough guys" out there that aren't worried about such things. Hunters feel an added sense of bravery when with a compadre, but put these tough guys out alone to hunt, and track in failing light, and I think many of them might act more like timid school girls. When you're actually doing it, it's a different story. When you've just climbed out of your stand in the early evening night after a hunt, and you know there is a sow with cubs near by because you watched them on the bait earlier, you can't help but feel a little uneasy. But it's this quickening of the pulse that makes the bear baiting experience so exciting.

I recall one year that I was baiting for a friend who came from out of state to hunt. I was carrying the bait in before work, and just as I dumped it out, I saw a black bear approaching. It's one of those sights you see in the wild, and never forget. This was a good size bear, and he emerged in stark contrast out of the bright green ferns with a foggy sort of a mist rising off the ground all around him due to the sun evaporating the early morning dew. He was about 30 yards away when I first spotted him, and he continued to slowly amble along sniffing the air, and looking off to his sides as he closed the distance. At about 15 yards, I drew my 44 magnum, and cocked it, thinking surely he's going to see the movement, and be on his way. Being less than ten yards from a rather large wild black bear by myself, I started to feel a bit nervous. I started to think that perhaps the bear knew I was there after all, and I was the bait today as he seemingly looked right through me. Before taking a bead on the bear at about eight yards, I started to rock my upper body in a back and forth motion just to confirm that he did indeed see me. He instantly swapped ends, and bolted in terror, so quick and unexpected was his movement that I actually jumped as well.

On another hunt I caught a bit of movement out of the corner of my eye. There was a little tiny cub walking up the same trail that I used to approach the bait sight. Somehow he sensed me because he nervously veered off the path in front of me staring straight ahead like a kid scared to glance in the corner because he just knows the boogey man is there. Once completely by me he broke into a dead run until out of sight. I never saw another bear that night, and it was one of those eerie walks out when you know momma isn't too far away. At that point, I knew what that scared cub felt like as he was afraid to glance over at me.

In the Solo Bear chapter, you'll read about a tracking job done in failing light, but I'll share another story with you now. I had mentioned that I was baiting a bear for a friend from out of state. The site I had him hunting was being slammed by multiple bears. As a result they seemed to be coming at all hours of the day because I think they were trying to get to the bait ahead of the competition. He had only two days to hunt the sight, so he decided to stay on stand for the entire day on both days. The first day we walked in together, and dropped off the bait. I showed him where the stand was, and told him I'd be back to get him at dark. He had a cell phone so if he got lucky he could call me at work. That evening I parked my truck within ear shot of the bait sight, and expected to hear a shot, but none came. After legal shooting light, I made my way in, and we walked back out together in the dark, at which time he shared with me that he had not seen a thing the entire day. This was quite surprising to me considering the sight was being competed for by more than one bear. It was only a hunch, but this told me that perhaps my hunter hadn't been as still or as quiet as he should have been.

When your sitting in a stand for ten hours at a time, it's tough to remain as still as you need to be for the entire duration. This is why I generally only recommend hunting the four or five hours before dark. By doing this you're maximizing your ability to sit still during the most prime hours of hunting.

After a talk about doing your best to sit still, I freshened the bait that had not been touched, and dropped him off for his second day of hunting. The entire day passed with no calls from my hunter. I again showed up a couple hours before dark, and rested my eyes for a while in my truck while listening for the report of my friend's firearm. I entered the woods as it started to get dark to retrieve Steve. About half way in I was taken by surprise as the quiet of the evening woods was permeated by a rifle blast. My pace quickened, and I was soon standing beneath Steve's tree. After helping him down he enlightened me that he had seen four bears on stand this afternoon. The first three, a sow and two cubs had come in around 5:00 and he had watched them for quite some time, and the last one presumably a large boar that he had just shot at. I had repeatedly warned that I did not want a sow with cubs to be shot, and was pleased that he had respected that wish.

The logs that I use to cover the bait are quite heavy, and as the cubs came in they had tugged, and pulled trying to move them. Steve was amazed at the power of the sow as she had scattered the heavy logs with one seemingly effortless swat of the paw. Steve seemed uncertain of his shot which was a little perplexing, but I assumed he was just being cautious. Where the bear had been standing there was a good smattering of blood confirming a hit. It was really getting dark now, and with the help of flashlights we took up the blood trail. That bear painted the first 50 yards of the forest red, and I was convinced that he was laid up just beyond the next blow down. Most of my experience had been with deer hunting, and any deer that had laid a blood trail as heavy as that was as good as dead.

In one hand I had my 44 magnum held out in front of me with my thumb on the hammer, and the other held a flashlight as I nervously inched my way along. It's nerve racking to say the least to be following a bear's blood trail in the dark; every little noise jangles your nerves. The trail stretched on further than I thought it would, and when the bear started up and over a ridge I knew things weren't good. Mortally wounded animals generally don't run uphill. When we started down over the other side of the ridge, the blood started to get sparse, and that bear climbed into the thickest, nastiest pile of jack firs you could imagine. The jack firs caught the beam of the flashlights, and the light would not permeate out in front of you. You basically could not see anything beyond arms reach. It was an eerie feeling to know if that wounded bear in front of us was laid up in this thick stuff we'd be on top of him before there was any time for a shot.

This bear had taken us quite some distance now, and being that it was pitch black I had no idea where we were. At this point the only option would be to walk out by compass. We were on our hands and knees now searching for spots of blood when the trail took us over a small water-filled slough that looked familiar. Turns out I had trapped a mink not far from here in prior years, and I realized that the slough would lead us to a larger river that we could follow out. The trail was getting so sparse now that we had only traveled an additional 50 yards beyond the slough in a half hour's time. I made the difficult decision to leave the blood trail and return in the morning with additional help.

The next morning Dad met us at first light, and the three of us took up the trail again. I'd like to say the story has a happy ending, but it doesn't. We lost the blood trail completely a few hundred yards beyond where we had left it the night before. We spent a considerable amount of time searching blindly, but to no avail. Unfortunately if you hunt long enough I believe at some time or another you will have a story to tell of a wounded animal. Though I can't say for sure, I believe this bear died.

Bears are a tough animal, and they are built differently than a deer. They are thicker, and more compact, and their bone structure is heavier. I also believe that their vitals sit slightly more forward than does a deer's. They are covered with a layer of fat that has a tendency to clog bullet holes which makes a wounded animal tough to follow. Their thick hair also absorbs a lot of blood which in combination with the fat clogging the bullet holes makes them even harder to follow. For all of these reasons I believe that even with a high-powered rifle you have to make sure your shot is perfect to the point that even a broad side shot is not good enough. Wait until that bear reaches forward with his paw, and exposes his lungs. Remember they sit slightly more forward than does a deer's. When his paw is forward, his heavy shoulder bone is also stretched forward to reveal more of the vitals. Your aiming point should be about midway between back bone and belly. The bear's long shaggy fur may lead you to believe his chest is deeper to the ground than it actually is.

I have hunted on a few unsuccessful guided bear hunts in northern Maine. Due to a guide's occupation I have reason to believe he's trailed a few wounded bears. One claimed that if you hit a bear's shoulder, and that bullet only penetrates one lung, that bear will run for miles, and you'll never find it. Therefore I think that you want a heavy bullet that's probably bonded so it's not going to blow apart upon hitting heavy bone at close range. You want that heavy bullet to pass all the way through leaving an exit wound. I want an exit wound on every animal I shoot. Even well hit deer are hard to blood trail if there is no exit wound. The bullet has expanded after hitting the animal, making the exit wound bigger, and thus dumping out more blood, not to mention that two holes dump more blood than one. I don't buy into the idea that a bullet should stop under the hide on the opposite side of the animal thereby using all of its energy within the animal.

Remember my story when I shot a nice buck straight through the heart with my grandfathers 30/30, and the bullet stopped under the hide on the opposite side. He only ran 80 yards, but it was in thick jack firs, and you could only see five to ten yards at a time. Even though the deer was hit perfectly, I thought I had missed since there was not a stitch of blood. The only way I could discern the deer's path was by making circles until I came upon the disturbed sand, and leaves where the bounding buck had landed, and again jumped. Sick to my stomach about missing a nice buck and nearly ready to give up on him, I stumbled onto the dead animal as I circled for the next set of running hoof prints in the leaves. I've had other similar experiences with well-hit animals not leaving a blood trail due to no exit wound, and have been in on hunts with others that have proven this point. In short you need to hit a bear right.

My experience has been that you either find a bear dead within 100 yards, or you don't find him. I can think of no stories even from others when a bear was trailed for any length of time, and then recovered. It's not to say that it can't happen, but this has just been my own personal experience.

When I told Lou Gagnon of my blood trailing job after dark, he mentioned that I might be a few bricks shy of a load. Save yourself the grief, and aggravation, and be prepared in every way before you attempt to kill a bear. It's only fair to the animal. Many marginally hit deer are recovered, not so with bear. This means hunting with a weapon that you're very familiar with, and burning through box's of ammunition. Shoot from a stand the same height as the stand you'll be hunting out of, and at a target the same distance away as your bait. This not only improves your shooting, but helps you mentally by becoming more confident.

Lou Gagnon and another Maine black bear.

If I could only give one single piece of advice to another hunter, I would say, learn how to shoot. Study your choice of bullets, and shoot the heaviest accurate load that you can in your rifle. In short, leave nothing to chance like the slob hunter that takes his rifle out of the closet for the first time that year, and goes hunting without shooting it. Sure these guys get lucky once in a while, but they usually have more stories about the ones that got away, or the ones they wounded. I even think that going out and taking a few shots before the season to check your gun's zero to make sure it's sighted in properly isn't good enough. At the very least a hunter should shoot every week for a month prior to the season.

Most years I start shooting in June, and continue until the season starts. Learning to shoot, and becoming thoroughly familiar with one's rifle is the greatest single thing a new hunter can do to improve his chances in the woods. It makes the physical action of shooting like second nature, and causes it to happen without thought. It also helps mentally. Only through confidence, and experience is one able to overcome buck fever. If enough time is spent in the woods, eventually you're going to get an opportunity, and if shooting is automatic, buck fever will be less of an issue as your "training" takes over and you make the shot. The skilled confident shooter kills more deer as missing one becomes less of an issue, and he is able to make difficult shots that others might not even try.

Now that I've talked a little about bear hunting in general, different methods, being prepared, and shot placement on a bear, I'm going to share a couple of bear hunting stories.

11

SOLO BEAR

I arrived at my tree stand a little after noon, and settled in. As the hours passed I grew impatient. I thought my bear had moved off to feed on greener pastures. I was considering abandoning the hunt as darkness was quickly approaching. I never heard a thing, but all at once a black apparition melted out of the hemlocks. He approached the hanging stink bag; this is a foul-smelling concoction used to pull bears in from long distances. He stood on his hind legs to inspect it with his nose. Without warning he switched ends in a bristling ball of black fur, and bolted through the forest.

It was uncanny, he never made a sound. It was as if someone had turned off the volume. He should have made noise, but his soft fur, and broad padded feet delivered him silently through the surrounding thick underbrush. My heart skipped a beat for a few seconds, but he soon came sneaky footing back in. This time, straight to the bait pile. He rolled the logs off. This forced him to pull from several different directions, just like I had intended. He offered several different, nice shot angles as my rifle lay helplessly across my lap. Not daring to move for fear of being detected, all I could do was sit and watch the bear work the bait.

TWELVE DAYS PRIOR

September 1st finally rolled around. The much anticipated start of the New Hampshire black bear baiting season had arrived. I was due to leave for a caribou hunt in two weeks. This cut the month-long baiting/hunting season in half for me. I was determined, just the same, to have a go at it.

A lot of different factors determine how quickly a bear will hit a bait sight. Bears range widely in the vast mountainous area of the White Mountain National Forest where my bait sight is located. If a bear is in the area, and at this time of year that depends largely on what food sources are naturally available, your bait sight is likely to get hit within a few days. If there are no bears in the immediate area, you could possibly bait for weeks before this elusive critter finally discovers your sight. If you've seen bear sign in the area, or have known bears to frequent the area, stay with it. Perseverance will pay off. A bear can follow a scent for a long way.

I like to put out something really putrid smelling to pull a bear in. He won't necessarily eat this, so you should have sweets waiting when he arrives. His stomach is his weakness, and the aromas wafting from your sight will eventually prove to be more than it can "bear" to ignore. I like to cover my bait with maybe one-half dozen large logs. This insures that when I return and find them strewn about, none other than Mr. Bruin is responsible.

THE BAIT

I use old bread and pastries for a base ingredient in my bait. I then take a few scoops of cracked corn, and black oil sunflower seeds, add them in, and then top the whole thing off with a gallon of commercial grade molasses. All of these items with the exception of the bread can be purchased at your local horse feeds supply fairly reasonably, and will make a sticky sweet mess that bears can't resist.

Other animals will inevitably track the sticky molasses out through the forest leaving a scent trail to your sight that will eventually attract a bear. You don't necessarily have to purchase these things to be successful. Be creative; bears will eat almost anything. Old frialator grease from your local restaurant will achieve the same objective that molasses will for laying down a scent trail to your sight once a raccoon gets his paws in it, and can usually be acquired for free.

A whole week passed without any sign of a bear. My bait sight had smaller animals, raccoons, etc. in the bait, tracking aromas out through the forest. Squirrels scampered about stashing away molasses-covered cracked corn in every nook and cranny, and I could smell my sight from 75 yards. It felt alive, and I knew it was only a matter of time, but with my caribou hunt quickly approaching, time was something I didn't have.

One of the secrets of baiting, especially when it starts being visited, is not to build up too much bait. If the bear has a ton of food, he feels as if he can waltz in, and eat anytime. We want him to come during daylight, so limit it to five gallons a night, even if there's multiple bears coming. If they think someone will get there ahead of them, they will start coming earlier. The two nights before you hunt, cut the five-gallon portion in half. This will really get them nervous with the idea that a competitor is raiding their cache. This serves to help pull nocturnal bears in a bit earlier.

STAND LOCATION

I like to locate my bait sight in a thick swampy area where a bear might feel comfortable moving about during daylight. Mine was located in a thick hemlock swamp where even on the sunniest of days the damp forest floor only dreams of being dappled with sunlight — it's a dark ominous looking area. The type of place that is removed from any trace of human activity. So much so that the lonely feeling of solitude creeps in. That feeling used to uncomfortably nag at me when I was younger, and hunting far from the blacktop, but I've since learned to thrive on it. When I get that feeling, I know I'm close to my quarry. My quarry shuns civilization, whether it be a cagey old loner of a whitetail or the elusive black bear. So when I'm in pursuit, I must learn to be like my prey.

"You'll have to leave the ways of the civilized world behind and learn to blend in with nature. You'll have to go wherever your instincts tell you to go without worrying about getting lost."
Hal Blood, **Hunting Big Woods Bucks**

A little secret is not to set your tree stand up on the trail you walk in on. When that bear comes into the bait, the first thing he's going to do is give a good hard look up the trail that you walked in on because he knows that's where the danger comes from. If you're sitting in your stand on that trail, and you're not perfectly still, he's going to pick up on you. If your stand is even 10 or 15 yards to the left or right of your entrance trail, the bear's attention is going to be drawn away from you, and could possibly afford you that little bit of extra movement when preparing for the shot. A small tip, but oftentimes it's the attention to these small details that means the difference between success or failure.

COVER SCENT

Finally get the bear used to a scent like anise oil when he starts coming. I freshen my anise oil every day when I drop the bait. Take the clothes you plan to hunt in, and seal them in a plastic trash bag with this same scent (vanilla works also). If your hunting clothes reek of this scent, it will not only cover your human odor, but it's like ringing the dinner bell to let any and all bears know that their meal has arrived. Last but not least, in my opinion, the perfect bear stand should have a small babbling brook or stream about 10 yards behind you. Not only for the sweet music it provides, but it will also help to conceal any small noises that you might accidentally make.

Black bears are often referred to as "black ghosts," because of the way they move silently through the woods, and their knack for not being seen by human eyes. Now you've learned to not be seen by setting your stand away from your entrance trail.

You've learned to evade detection from being smelled by covering your human odor with anise, or vanilla, and you've learned how to become completely silent by covering any small noise that you might make while shifting your weight, with the gurgling brook. You as well now, must become invisible, and the bear is no longer the only ghost in the woods. You've maximized your chances for seeing that bear.

BACK TO THE STORY

On the eighth day of baiting, I was toting a five-gallon pail full of sweets with the fading hope that a bruin had pulled the heavy logs away, and devoured my bait. Half way in, where I cross a small, freestone brook that babbles quietly and cold, straight out of the mountains, I noticed a track in the sand. Upon closer inspection, I discovered one single perfect front paw print from a bear. Not a huge print, but my pace quickened just the same. I knew before I got there what I was going to find. The bait sight was torn up. The way it was ripped apart with such careless abandon, and judging by the track size, I figured the bear to be a young male about 150 pounds Dressed weight. A perfect bear to harvest and, in my eyes, a trophy.

I only had six days to hunt before my trip. My business was keeping me very busy trying to tie up loose ends before I left for the caribou hunt, and I had an ultrasound with my wife to see our first child (a baby girl). With all of this going on, I still managed to drop my bait early each morning, and I carefully devised, calculated and schemed a plan to allot myself at least one afternoon of actual hunting before I headed north. It happened to fall two days ahead of my departure.

Full of enthusiasm, I arrived at my bait sight the morning of my hunt. I was shocked to see my bait had not been hit the previous night. I somewhat disappointedly left the bait, and started to question my intentions of returning at noon to hunt. Later that morning it began to rain, and doubt seriously started to creep in. Shooting a bear in one afternoon of hunting seemed like a long shot, but I decided to follow through on my plans. One thing the outdoors has taught me is perseverance, and persistence more often than not pays off.

All the thousands of hours spent in the woods hunting, trapping, and fishing, and I've never seen a black bear other than at my bait sights. Eventually, if enough time is spent outdoors, mother nature will slowly teach you, sometimes so slowly that you don't notice over the years, subtle lessons, but she will eventually give up her most prized secrets.

Finally to get back to where I left off at the opening paragraph when I was watching the bear while my rifle lay helplessly across my lap — The bear finally grabbed a doughnut, and sauntered off to eat it. That was all the chance I needed to ready my rifle, and when he returned, from my right, he reached forward with his left leg to pull at the bait pile. The crosshairs quickly found his shoulder. The report of my rifle sent him fleeing like greased lightning, and this time not so quietly. He uttered a low guttural growl as he bolted through the undergrowth, a sound that sent chills down my spine and the hair on the back of my neck stood up.

I took my time getting down from my stand. I considered going to get help, but that would mean tracking a bear in pitch black (not my favorite pastime). I felt confident in my shot, so I decided to go it alone. Your nerves have a way of wearing on you when following a bear's blood trail by yourself in fading light. I crept along, all of my senses on full alert. I had swapped my 30/06 for my faster handling 44 magnum revolver. I was thinking that a deer would have given out long ago with such a heavy blood trail. The blood was however starting to get a little more sparse, and I was starting to get a little more worried.

This bear was taken on a solo hunt by the author.

Darkness was upon me. I was scanning the forest floor with a small flashlight attached to my key chain, looking for the next splotch of blood, when my narrow beam of light picked up solid black. With my heart in my throat I nervously cocked the 44, and jerked it out in front of me. Holding the heavy gun at arms length with one hand, I noticed how much I was shaking. There standing out against the light green ferns, and nestled against a clump of jack firs was my sleek jet black prize. The sky had cleared, and I looked up through the leaf work at the starlit night sky and gave thanks. I quickly dressed the bruin, and dragged him several hundred yards to a beaver flowage I had trapped out the previous year. I knew I could find my way back here in the dark with someone to help drag.

I had been on several unsuccessful guided bear hunts to northern Maine in previous years, but looking back, I'm glad they were unsuccessful. Those hunts don't give you the chance to run the bait yourself, and feel the anticipation of checking your bait sight every day — sneaking in like a kid in a candy store to see what's taken place. You feel the excitement of discovering that your bait sight has been hit, and the thrill of not knowing exactly where that bruin is each day when you approach the bait sight. He could be a mile away, or he could be hidden mere feet away in the thick of the swamp. It's very rewarding when you catch that first unsuspecting glimpse of an ever elusive black. Taking a bear on public land that I baited, and hunting solo in my home state, and knowing I did it by myself is very satisfying, and an adventure unparalleled at any cost. If you have the opportunity, get out and give it a try this fall.

This story was originally printed in *Fur-Fish-Game* magazine. It's my all-time favorite outdoor magazine. I'm not being paid in any way to say this, but I truly feel that it is loaded with advice for the practical outdoorsman, the every-day-working-class-hunter. I've learned more from *Fur-Fish-Game* than probably all the other magazines combined — it's that good. I think that some of the other outdoor magazines are getting out of touch with the average hunter. When you give advice concerning a 50,000 dollar African safari, I don't think the average hunter can relate to that. It's enjoyable to read about such adventures on occasion, but there comes a point when you loose touch with the average man. If you're a hard-working, honest, decent, family man, you will fit into my circle of friends just fine — no question. If you're into clicks, and whose got the biggest truck, and the latest and greatest gear, then it's not so much about the outdoor experience, and then the other magazines are right up your alley. The "TV hunters" that constantly drop the names of their big sponsors are all sitting under a game feeder down in Texas behind a really big fence. They can be found in a lot of magazines. They are really "cool" and looking for followers to buy into their hype. Don't be a follower, be a leader. The true woodsman grounded in the earth will for sure find a connection to *Fur-Fish-Game* magazine.

"You have noticed that everything an Indian does is in a circle, and that is because the power of the world always works in circles, and everything tries to be round…The sky is round, and I have heard that the earth is round like a ball, and so are all the stars. The wind in it's greatest power, whirls. Birds make their nests in circles, for theirs is the same religion as ours…Even the seasons form a great circle in their changing, and always come back again to where they were. The life of a man is a circle from childhood to childhood, and so it is in everything where power moves."

~ Black Elk Ogala Sioux

12

FULL CIRCLE

I had been on two separate guided bear hunts in northern Maine. The two hunts were swapped for my talents as a woodcarver. They were week-long hunts. I would carve each day until about 1:00 in the afternoon, and the rest of the day would be spent watching over a bear bait. The bare wooden seats on the homemade stands were rough on the backside at six hours to a sitting. In two weeks of hunting nary a bear was spotted. The outfitter's lodge was nicely decorated with woodcarvings, and I was nicely decorated with itching red bumps after supporting the mosquito population for a week at a time. Besides some new friendships, and an education in bear baiting, all I had gained was a sore butt, and mosquito bites.

I decided to try my hand at bear baiting right in my home state of New Hampshire. The Maine hunts, I came to find out, just weren't meant to be. The good lord had something different, and better in mind for me. The idea of taking a black ghost who haunted the same woods as me was very appealing. A bear who called home the vast mountainous forest of the Chocorua valley, and a bear that drinks from the same cold mountain flows that I learned to trap in. A bear that roams the rugged terrain like an apparition, and each day as the sun sets behind the Mountains to the west is swallowed by the shadow of Mt. Chocorua, and its dark secrets. My woodshop lies at the very mouth of the valley. The Chocorua River gets its start in the uppermost reaches of the mountain, and empties out into civilization mere yards from my shop.

Mount Chocorua's jagged summit as viewed from Chocorua Lake.

The almost 4000-foot craggy peak that juts its rocky summit well above tree line was named after Chief Chocorua. The story of Chief Chocoura and his son who called home the valley where my carving shop is now located is a tragic one.

When the area was first being settled, most of the Indians in the area were driven out by the white settlers, and most of them moved north to Canada. Chief Chocorua, and his beloved son stayed in the area as the chief trusted and had a good rapport with one of the well respected local white families, the Campbells. The chief was called away on a long trip, and entrusted his son with Mr. Campbell, who was also a trapper, and the only white that he trusted enough to protect his son in his absence. While the chief was gone, his son got into some of Mr. Campbells poison trapping bait, which caused his death. When the chief returned he did not believe that it was an accident, and in a rage murdered the entire Campbell family. The white settlers formed a posse and hunted the chief who vowed he would not be killed by a white man. They trailed him to the top of the mountain where he jumped from a rocky cliff to his death, but not before uttering a curse on the white men who dared settle the valley below.

**The bearskin rug that was the result of the "Full Circle" hunt.
Displayed at my woodshop along with some of my handiwork.**

September first finally arrived, and with it the first day of bear baiting/hunting. I had already chosen a baiting site, and hung a stand not far from my carving store. The short distance from my workshop would make it easy to drop the bait at lunch time each day. I must have chosen my sight well, because within a few days the bait not only was hit, but torn to shreds by an aggressive bear. I continued to run the bait for another week in an attempt to get the bear into a pattern. To my surprise, I discovered by checking the bait after work at 5:00-6:00 that the bear had often already been there. I started to feel a little more lucky.

The day finally arrived for me to hunt. I arrived at my sight around noon as usual, this time clad with camouflage, and my 30/06 hunting rifle. After freshening the bait, I climbed into my stand approximately 30 yards away. I had positioned the bait against a giant van-size boulder so the bear would have to walk along its side, and offer a broadside shot. I was in my stand for about 40 minutes when I heard some twigs snap off to my left. It was a brief distraction, and I soon forgot about it.

As I sat on stand the air was dry, and a steady cool breeze caused the surrounding trees to sway. I was carried back in thought to some of my earliest memories as a child at my grandparent's camp in Pittsburgh, New Hampshire I can see the white birch, and poplar trees bending, dappling filtered light through there many shades of green leaves. The tall grass outside the camp swayed in the cool early summer wind. I was in the middle of it all with my grandfather by my side telling me to keep my elbow tucked in as I practiced casting his fly rod. Pittsburgh is a small town up near the Canadian border. The entrance to the camp was located on the far side of the headwaters of the Connecticut river. Once across the river it was a three-quarter mile hike uphill before arriving at camp. The camp was equipped with gravity fed water out of a small nearby brook, gas lights and an outhouse.

The deer are sparse up in these big woods, but they make up in size what they lack in numbers. The bucks typically have short thick antlers, and a trophy is judged by it's 200-pound or heavier field-dressed body weight. The long brutal winters weed out the weak of the species, and as a result, a larger, tougher breed of "warrior" deer is produced. Nature is cruel, and in the natural world only the strong survive. One spring at camp my grandfather took me for a walk through the woods. Not far from camp we found a stout set of shed antlers lying side by side. The antlers carried heavy bases, and eight points. My grandfather gave me the antlers. Those antlers survived numerous moves from house to house, and a four-year move to Georgia while my father completed college. They were also used for dozens of trips into the woods for use as rattling antlers by myself, and with friends. Bucks use their antlers to fight one another for dominance and breeding rights. By rattling antlers together in the woods, occasionally a dominant buck can be lured in to exert his dominance, and breed the doe that's being "fought" over. Somehow those antlers always managed to stick around.

As I got older, the antlers started to take on more of an important symbolism for me, and I began to keep closer tabs on them. They reminded me of my grandfather, my love of deer hunting, and my carefree youth. As time went on, I also learned that I liked to work with my hands, and the thought of crafting one of the antlers into a knife came to me.

At first, I kind of rejected the idea thinking that it would almost be sinful to cut the antlers apart, but in time I became at peace with the idea, and soon thought that it would be the right thing to do. I even started to cherish the idea of carrying, on my side, the antler of a warrior buck that lived and fought in such a wild wilderness. The antler handle would hold so many memories, and so much meaning, as well. I did make the knife, and it has accompanied me on many hunts. I attached to it, with a piece of rawhide, a coyote claw. My thinking was that it would remind me to be elusive, and invisible while seeking out my prey like the coyote. I also inlayed a golden deer track into the base of the antler where it attached to the bucks head.

I used gold, which I had spent all summer digging out of a New Hampshire river on my days off. At the end of the summer I had a new appreciation for the prospectors of old as this is very back breaking work for little reward. The knife even survived being lost in the woods last season. I had killed a large doe with my muzzleloader, and after gutting her, misplaced the knife at some point. I scoured the area for hours to no avail. I returned home to my wife with the doe, but a normally joyous occasion was dulled by the sick feeling in my gut over the knife. The next day my wife returned with me to the area, and we quickly found it within 15 minutes of reaching the kill site.

I had quenched its blade with the blood of every furbearer, and big game animal in new England, including moose, with the exception of the elusive black bear. The thought kept running through my mind that harvesting a bear would bring things full circle.

I came back to reality as I heard the twigs snap again, and I touched my knife out of habit to be reassured of its presence. About that time, the black face of my much anticipated prize appeared from the thick fir trees just beyond the rock. He peered up the trail I normally take in, and then proceeded right to the bait pile. As he pulled at the logs I had placed, he finally offered me just the right angle. My rifle roared, and the bear uttered a low growling as he made two leaps backward in a glistening black ball of fur. In the time it took me to operate the bolt action on my rifle and train it on the bear again, he already lay dead not 15 yards from my tree. A quick kill affords a fine memory of such a hunt, but one that takes mere seconds is truly something to be proud of.

I noticed that I felt close to the land, and a part of something that all the old time hunters, and trappers and even native people had once been a part of in this very forest. Modern society and stresses disappeared if only for a moment. I know that a lifetime is short, and I will probably soon be forgotten as those that went before me, but the wind will quietly whisper through the trees in its subtle way the epic tales of adventure that have played out through the years in the shadow of Mt. Chocorua, for all of those close enough to the earth, and in tune enough with nature to hear.

I cut one of the front claws from the bear, and attached it to my knife by drilling a hole in the antler base, and running rawhide between the two. Several weeks passed, and I again examined the knife, and claw. There are a couple of abnormal points that stick off the base of the antler that were rubbed smooth, and polished so many years ago by the antlers original owner. These points together with the claw formed a perfect circle. It was a moment of clarity when I realized, that even at a very young age God had a plan for me by finding the antlers. He knew that I was going to become a craftsman, and sculptor, and create a knife with them and that I was going to own a shop in this valley — even that I was going to kill this bear, not in Maine, but when the timing, and circumstances were right, here in New Hampshire. A series of events throughout the course of my life had been linked together, and fallen in place in such a way, in my mind, as to be undeniable.

The "Full Circle" bear.

My hunting knife and the heavy set of shed antlers it was created from.

13

CREATE YOUR OWN DEER ANTLER HUNTING KNIFE

From the time the first cave dweller broke a rock and used the jagged edge as a cutting device, man has been intrigued with knives. Of all the possessions that I bring with me on the hunt, including my rifle, I'd have to say that my knife is the most prized. I've gained much satisfaction from making my own hunting knife and I would like to help the reader to do the same. I think that everyone should, at one time, feel the satisfaction that comes from creating something useful with their own hands. The Native Americans and all indigenous peoples created their own tools. Therefore, to create a useful tool with your own hands that is instrumental in the hunting process is a link to the hunters of old who depended on their hunting skills and tools to sustain life. It will make one feel more a part of the natural world and closer to the natural order of the food chain — animals of the hunt. It will also lend to a feeling of self-sufficiency.

Diagrams A, B, and C show the progression of the knife building process. Notice the shape of the holes in both the antler handle, and the finger guard. The x in diagram C shows the approximated placement of the pin to lock the knife blade in place.

Diagram A

Diagram B

Diagram C

Materials:

Deer antler

Knife blade (knife maker's supply)

Brass bar stock (knife maker's supply)

Brass pin (knife maker's supply)

Two-ton epoxy (purchased at any hardware store)

Texas knife maker's supply toll free: 1-888-461-8632

Tools:

Hand held power drill

Round file (chainsaw file)

Small flat files of numerous shapes with pointed ends

Bench grinder

Soldering kit

It is my opinion that this knife can be built cheaply, with very basic tools, and a minimal amount of skill. Most readers will probably already have the basic tools required to complete this project. The first order of business is to obtain an antler for use as the handle. I say a deer antler, but it could be moose, caribou or any other piece of antler that you choose. If enough time is spent in the woods, most hunters will eventually find a shed antler of some type. You may even choose an antler from a buck that either you or a family member has killed. The more "significance" the antler has, the more cherished the knife will be when carried on your belt and put to use.

Once you've found an antler the next step is to select a blade. Anyone who wants to get a little more involved can make their own blade, but for now I recommend that you purchase a pre-made blade from a knife making supply company as I did. I recommend Texas Knife Maker's Supply.

The reason I recommend this company is because they offer cryogenically treated knife blades. Cryogenically treated means that the steel has been frozen at minus 305 degrees below zero (Fahrenheit). Believe me, this is worthwhile. This steel holds an edge better than any knife I've ever owned. The difference in the edge holding ability between this treated steel, and the knife bought over the counter is extremely dramatic — you will notice a difference. If you purchased a knife for several hundred dollars you might possibly get this quality, but I've always been a 25-to-50-dollar-knife-kind-of a guy, and truthfully, probably closer to 25 dollars. Spending any more than that on a knife always seemed "frivolous" to me.

You can just purchase the cryogenically treated blade for around 25 dollars. I processed (gutted, quartered, and some meat slicing) four deer in New York last fall, and two more here in New Hampshire without sharpening the knife. Granted it was getting pretty dull toward the end of it, but the knives I've owned in the past would have needed sharpening after the first deer, and most certainly after the second. For me hunting season is a whirlwind between work, family and hunting. If a knife doesn't absolutely need sharpening, it will take a back seat until after the season ends.

A hunting knife blade should not be any longer than four or five inches. Believe me when I tell you that any more than that will just be getting in the way. It should thicken a little at the edge furthest from the cutting edge — the back of the blade. This is for durability while in heavy use — splitting the pelvic bone would be a good example.

The last thing that I will mention about blade selection is to try and find a blade whose curve complements that of the antler handle. Take notice how the flowing "s" curve is formed between the steel and the antler in the knives pictured. While ordering the blade, you should also order some bar stock for the finger guard. This bar stock should be nickel-silver if you like a silver looking finger guard, and brass if you like a gold look, both of these materials work easily with a file. You should order a piece of matching metal rod to pin through the antler handle and the tang of the knife (the long skinny part sticking off of the blade) to help hold the blade securely in place.

Start by drilling a hole slightly larger than the tang into the antler handle with a hand-held power drill. Now take a round file (chainsaw file) and try to make the perfectly round hole created by the drill bit a little more oval. This insures that when the knife tang is set in the two-ton epoxy it will never want to spin in the hole. You could stop here and add the epoxy, and have a very usable knife, but I recommend adding the metal rod through the tang and handle to help keep the knife's tang from spinning in the antler handle. Also the finger guard should be added for safety, and because it adds to the eye appeal as well.

If your going to proceed further, you should drill a hole through the bar stock that is slightly smaller than the tang. Now using small, flat hand files, try to make the hole square to fit as closely as possible over the tang of the knife. Any gaps here will be noticeable in the finished product, so take your time. Once the bar stock fits nicely over the tang and buts up against the blade, you will need to solder it in place. In order to avoid ruining the temper of the blade by heating it in the soldering process, I submerge the blade in a coffee can full of water suspended by a pair of vice grips so that the tang section to be soldered is sticking out above the water.

The next problem will be drilling a hole through the hardened steel tang. You can buy an expensive drill bit, or you can heat the tang to cherry red during the soldering process to ruin the temper or soften the steel. The last option, which is my preferred method, is to get a buddy who works in a machine shop to do it. They can perform this task easily. If you're going to do it yourself, you should clamp the blade solidly to the drill press and run the drill through the desired spot on the tang. Without moving the tang, slide the antler knife handle over the tang, and hold it there with your hand. Now run the drill bit down again, this time it will cut a hole in the antler handle then proceed through the "already cut" hole in the tang, and on through the other side of the antler handle. The alignment will be perfect, and after adding the two-ton epoxy you can go ahead and drive in the metal rod to pin the knife blade in place. Trim the metal rod slightly longer than it should be so it sticks a little bit out both sides of the knife handle. Hammer these ends so they mushroom slightly, and this will prevent the metal pin from ever moving.

Once the two-ton epoxy has cured, go ahead and shape the square bar stock finger guard to whatever shape you desire. Power sanders work great for shaping the metal, but hand files will also do the trick, just a little more slowly. Start by shaving the metal down until it is following the shape of the antler that it rests against. You want the finger guard to be a metal cap, or extension of the antler handle. Once that is achieved, you can shape the finger guard down to the typical point. Feel free to look at my knife for inspiration.

After everything is the right shape, go ahead and polish the metal and antler. A good method to do this is to replace the stone on a bench grinder with a round felt pad. While the grinder is running, press jewelers polishing compound (also available through knife makers supply) against the felt pad. Now apply your antler handle, and finger guard to the felt pad after it has been "charged" with polishing compound. You will begin to see the scratches, and tool marks start to disappear, and the antler, and metal will start to polish to a shine, and mirror finish. Repeat the process until desired results are achieved.

My hand built hunting knife in the sheath that I also created alongside the newly created knife.

The last thing that I will talk about is a sheath for your knife. I built my own sheath, but the knife maker's supply sells pre-made sheaths that fit most of the blades that they sell. If you do decide to make your own sheath, I advise you to use hard leather that is joined with rivets. This is for safety purposes. If you make a sheath out of soft leather, and you fall in the woods, the knife is liable to cut through the soft leather, and possibly you too. I built my sheath out of hard leather, and then wrapped it in soft leather to add eye appeal.

14

SIT OR WALK?

There often seems to be a great debate on whether to sit or still hunt. To still hunt is actually the opposite of how it sounds. It's when you walk, or slowly hunt your way through the woods from one point to another. The camps (sit/walk) seem to be divided right down the middle, and according to many hunters, you're either one or the other. I can think of one hunter who I've come to enjoy hunting with a great deal. When we were first getting acquainted, he seemed to constantly slam the guys that like to sit, and especially the guys that used tree stands. He is an excellent still hunter, and has even taken several deer with a recurve bow while still hunting. When he asked me if I like to walk or sit, my reply was that I like to do both. At the time, it was as if he couldn't comprehend this, and he seemed to assume that I must be a sitter, and that I was just too ashamed to admit it.

Why is it so hard for some hunters to realize that both methods can be used? The truth is that I use both methods, and enjoy both. Depending on the hunting sign, conditions, and situation, I capitalize on whatever method makes the most sense. Each style has its own advantages and disadvantages. To limit yourself to just sitting or just walking is a huge disadvantage to my way of thinking. If you become proficient with both methods, you're a more well-rounded and skilled hunter, and after processing the hunting conditions, you have more "weapons" in your arsenal.

My way of thinking is: I will do whatever it takes to be successful. People's hunting styles rub off on each other, and after hunting with the previously mentioned still hunter, he has acquired several tree stands, and seems to recognize the advantage of sitting on occasion, though he remains mostly a still hunter.

The three things that get hunters busted by the deer are movement made by the hunter, sound made by the hunter, and most of all human scent emitted by the hunter. I always feel that my best chances of taking a deer are when I can eliminate at least two of these three factors, for example when it's windy, it's hard for the deer to hear the still hunter, or see the still hunter's movement.

That being said, my favorite time that I like to still hunt is when the woods are wet, maybe it's raining lightly, or misting. These conditions seem to keep my human scent down, and keep it from spreading around. I can slip along very quietly in these conditions, and what little noise I make is generally covered by the sound of the constant dripping of the moisture falling from the trees. I've all but eliminated two of the deer detecting factors in these conditions.

The third factor, the movement is kept to a minimum as well by frequently stopping to watch. You can tell when deer sign is smoking fresh in these conditions, because it quickly erodes due to the precipitation if it is not fresh. When I'm in these conditions and come upon fresh sign, I slow down to a snail's pace, I know that a deer could be wandering through at any time. I take a few steps, and stop to watch, always being careful not to be caught in the wide open. I'll always stop next to a tree, or something that breaks up my outline, and doubles as a solid place to plant my forearm against should the need to shoot arise. This may seem like a small detail, but small details are what put tags on deer. I may spend as much as 10 or 15 minutes in one place just watching before slowly moving another five or ten yards.

STILL HUNTING ADVANTAGES

The advantage of walking is that your constantly covering ground. Examples of when this might be an advantage would be at midday when animals are not moving much, or if the conditions are really windy. Deer get nervous in windy conditions, and bed down, they can't hear danger, scents are constantly swirling in the air currents, and they can't tell what direction they are coming from. Everything is constantly moving around them, and this makes it harder for them to detect movement of predators, and ultimately makes them more wary. If the deer are bedded, and your sitting still, you have zero chance of seeing them. Another example would be in a big woods area where the deer are sparse, if there's not a concentration of sign in any one spot, you increase your odds greatly by covering more ground. Only a knuckle head would sit still in the previously mentioned conditions.

STILL HUNTING DISADVANTAGES

Now that we know some of the advantages, of still hunting, and what conditions are best for still hunting, I'll talk about some of the disadvantages of still hunting. One of the disadvantages is that you are constantly moving, and even in the best of conditions, your still going to get busted by more deer than you are going to get a crack at. A hunt that comes to mind took place in a steady rain, as I slowly still hunted the top of a hardwood ridge, I came upon fresh deer tracks that were fairly easy to follow due to the overturned and disturbed leaves. The deer seemed to be walking, and despite my constant scrutiny of the woods in front of me, they still saw me before I saw them. They blew out of a small

133

clump of firs in front of me, and flags waving, were gone down over the backside of the ridge before I could get lined up on one. The thing of interest to me was that they had split up, with one deer running left, and the other more to the right as they went down over the ridge. I'll come back to this story a little later in the chapter.

Another disadvantage of still hunting is that your going to be shooting at moving, and even running deer a good deal of the time, and your generally not going to have much time to process the situation, you have to shoot quickly. Another situation when it would be a disadvantage to walk would be when the leaves are extremely crunchy, and you can hear a pin drop in the woods. Your going to spook any animals long before you see them, but if you prescribe to the knuckle head way of thinking that the only way to hunt is to walk, then you'll spend a lot of time helping other hunters that are smart enough to sit in these conditions to get their deer.

ADVANTAGES OF SITTING

Now that we've covered the advantages, and disadvantages of still hunting, I'll talk about some of the advantages of sitting. I mentioned that I like to try and eliminate at least two of the ways that deer can detect me while I'm hunting. When you take a stand, or sit still, you immediately eliminate movement and noise. This just leaves you with your human scent to worry about. I don't necessarily prescribe to the way of thinking that a tree stand puts your scent stream up in the air above the deer.

As an example, I like to watch the wood smoke coming out of my chimney. Some days it seems to drift straight up in the air and away, I can't smell it no matter where I stand around my house. I'd say a lot more frequently, I can smell it as soon as I leave my front door. This is why I think scent control is important. Despite the chimney's elevated position the scent of the smoke frequently finds it's way to the ground. I always hang my hunting clothes out in the fresh air when I'm not wearing them, and use a cover scent. Another advantage of sitting is that oftentimes you get to shoot at relaxed deer that are standing still, and can wait for the best shot angles, which reduces wounding deer.

The die-hard walkers usually argue that still hunting is more challenging. I even had one guy knock me for taking a stand with my bow, which I do eight out of ten times while bow hunting. His argument was that it's more challenging to still hunt with a bow. My reply was that bow hunting deer where I hunt is hard enough, why would I want to make it even more challenging?

I don't necessarily think that one method is easier than another, anyway. If you just pick a spot in the woods, and sit on a stump you're probably not going to be very lucky. The challenge is in scouting, and reading sign, and positioning yourself to take advantage. Most of the die-hard-walkers will readily admit that they don't have the patience to sit still for very long, and that boredom soon takes over. Well, if they were truly looking for an added challenge, then I should think sitting would be part of their primary hunting method.

I have to admit that sitting is a challenge for me, especially when it goes beyond a couple of hours, but I will do what I feel that I have to do to be successful. One of the times that I think it is advantageous to sit is when there is a good amount of fresh deer sign in a concentrated area. Why walk through the area, risk spooking the deer, and ultimately make them more difficult to hunt? You can be relatively sure that with a little bit of persistence in your stand hunting these deer will walk right by you, and likely present you with an easy standing still shot.

As far as sitting is concerned, I don't think that the weather conditions are as important as they are with still hunting, You can have good luck sitting in almost all weather conditions, with the exception of maybe strong winds. The biggest disadvantage of sitting still is that the deer could be doing the same thing, and your chances of seeing them are zero. Beyond that, I really don't think there are too many more disadvantages to sitting.

ADVANTAGE OF MASTERING BOTH STAND, AND STILL HUNTING

While still hunting in the steady rain, two deer, that I mentioned earlier, had jumped down over the ridge and split up, with one going to the right and the other to the left. Those deer were traveling together, and socializing together for a reason. Would they go their separate ways and have no interest in traveling together ever again since I had split them up? Of course not, and I knew that they would try and locate each other as soon as there hearts stopped hammering a little bit.

I proceeded down over the ridge directly in the middle of where the two deer had split up and run. I came to a hemlock swamp about halfway down the backside of the ridge, and figured this is about where the deer probably stopped running and proceeded walking. I picked a spot where I could see for a good 75 to 100 yards down in front of me, and sat down backed up against an enormous old hemlock tree.

I had nearly eliminated my noise, and scent due to the wet conditions, which is what made still hunting make sense. Now I decided to sacrifice my mobility with the third and final way that a deer could detect me by sitting still. I didn't have to wait long. About 15 or 20 minutes later one of the does came sneaky footing across about 50 yards down in front of me. Cold souls (the name I have assigned to my rifle) knocked her flat.

This is a good example of how to use sitting as well as still hunting to your advantage in a single morning of hunting. If I were strictly a stand hunter, I would have never jumped the deer as I would have likely been in a tree stand somewhere. If I had been of the mind that I never sit still, and am constantly on the move, I likely wouldn't have spent the 20 minutes leaning against the tree, and ultimately killing the deer. As I still hunted the ridge, the deer did not hear me due to the rain, and I don't believe that they smelled me because of how close I was able to approach before I blew them out of the firs. I had successfully eliminated two of the ways the deer were able to detect me, and this is why I was able to see them in the first place. As I sat leaning against the tree, I eliminated movement, and noise, and believe, as a result, I killed a deer.

THE WILD CARD — SCENT CONTROL

Of the three ways a deer can detect you, human scent is the toughest obstacle to overcome in the deer woods. It's the one wild card that can get you busted no matter if you sit or walk. A lot of inexperienced hunters that are not yet adept at reading deer signs often don't know how close they actually are to the animals, and don't get to see them because they've been winded. If the wind blew in a reliable, and steady direction, it would be easier to deal with, but most of the time the wind is swirling, and changing directions where I hunt. Some people completely ignore any need to control their scent with the theory that they will never eliminate it completely — so why bother. This is a mistake. Realizing that I can never completely eliminate my scent, I still try to control it as much as possible.

A good example that comes to mind is my wife's grandmother. Alyssa lived with her grandparents while growing up, and I used to frequently visit her at her grandparent's house. Being an older woman her grandmother was quite particular about how things around her home are, and an adult deer is no different. As a matter of fact, gram used to comment about what the cat had dragged in occasionally when I would visit. I can remember several occasions when the issue of dog pooh, or might I say the aroma of dog pooh, had arisen. If she thought she could detect the smell, she would mill about nervously with her eyes glancing at the floor. Not sure if her nose was fooling her, she might ask if any one else could smell something funny, and might go so far as to ask people to check their shoes.

I can remember one occasion (thank God it wasn't me) when one of Alyssa's friends came over, and gram immediately flew into a red-faced rage, as the foul ripe smelling stench of fresh dog feces was undeniable. The poor girl had unknowingly tracked it in across the carpet, and visual confirmation was not needed, the smell was immediately offensive, and immediately sent gram into full alarm.

Deer are very much the same. Most deer are somewhat used to smelling people at some time or another, whether it be hikers, or smells wafting through their territory from roadways, or residential areas. A faint smell of human scent may cause them concern, but not necessarily alarm. They may hesitate, and search for visual, or audible confirmation, some of this depends on whether the deer have already been under high pressure from hunters. If a deer gets a strong nose full of human scent, they will undoubtedly go on full alert, and seek to flee the undeniable danger. If you're careful with your scent, and keep your clothes aired out, and use a cover scent, this could be the difference between the deer picking up trace smells of you, and getting a strong nose full of fear. As I've said before it's the culmination of small details that put tags on deer.

I recommend washing your hunting clothes in an unscented detergent regularly, and letting them air dry. I generally will keep my outer clothes in a plastic bin with some crushed up hemlock boughs, and maybe even some fresh deer droppings until I exit my vehicle at the area to be hunted. I also use a generous dose of cover scent of my own making, especially around my hat.

LEARN FROM NATURES PREDATORS

I like to look at nature, and how she has designed her predators, some are constantly on the prowl like the coyote moving and using their noses to sniff out prey, such as rodents, and then digging them out of their holes. Others lie in wait at a strategic location like an owl waiting in ambush over a field using its elevated position, and excellent eyesight to ambush an unsuspecting rodent. Both predators are successful at killing the very same prey using different techniques. Is one right or wrong? Or is one animal better than the other due to it's hunting style? As humans, we have the ability to reason, and to take advantage of both types of hunting, and I for one do just that.

A typical hunt for me starts out with me sitting for a couple of hours at first light, and then getting up, and walking there after. I'm constantly aware of the wind whether sitting or moving. My first deer was killed still hunting, and I've killed many sitting still, as well as a few from a tree stand. The bottom line is, don't be a knucklehead and try to argue that walking is the only acceptable method or vice versa. Try to eliminate at least two of the three ways a deer can detect you, hunt according to the conditions and the sign present. Sure there is a little bit of luck involved no matter what, but by eliminating two of the ways a deer can detect you, you've greatly tipped the odds in your favor. Be a well rounded and knowledgeable hunter, and master as many styles of hunting as you can. You will be prepared to take advantage of whatever situations arise, and, ultimately, you will be a more successful hunter.

A good and affordable way to produce your own cover scent is a process known as tincturing. You need a five-gallon bucket with a lid that has the rubber seal on it. Stuff the bucket as cram packed full as you can with some type of material with a scent typical of where you hunt. One of my favorite cover scents is hemlock, so I would stuff the bucket full of hemlock bows. After the bucket is full, I then dump a half gallon of vodka over the contents of the bucket, seal it and wait for one year. The high alcohol content in the vodka is what is needed for the tincture process, and the alcohol actually becomes whatever is in the bucket. No other preserving is needed. The vodka has no real smell of it's own, and it's an all natural way, with all natural ingredients to produce a cover scent that comes directly from the woods that you hunt in. You'll never reproduce that with anything that you buy over the counter. If you want to make an earth scent, you can use leaves, and the earthy smelling matter that is under them, or birch bark, oak leaves, etc., or whatever else you think would cover your scent effectively. When you're ready to use it, you can buy a cheap spray bottle for less than a dollar that will spray a fine mist.

15

GEAR LIST

Ilike to wear a backpack when I hunt. I know, I can hear the old timers already barking at me about carrying more stuff than I need, and lugging it around in a bulky pack. The truth is that I probably don't carry much more than they do. Instead of stuffing big pockets, my items are neatly organized on my back. I feel that it makes me more streamlined, more agile and more versatile. I don't wear a full sized backpack, but a smaller more streamlined pack. The chain store, Cabela's has lots of models to choose from. Take your time and make a well-thought-out purchase. Pick one that is quiet in the woods, waterproof, and light weight. Most important is that it should have little clips that connect the shoulder straps in front of your chest. You don't want to get into a frustrating situation where your shoulder straps keep slipping off your shoulders. Another feature you might look for is a piece of orange cloth that pulls out of a zipper, and hangs down over the pack to meet the laws that some states have regarding inches of exposed hunter orange. My pack does have this feature. Most of the time the main compartment in my backpack is completely empty. How's that for lugging around too much stuff?

Most hunting books, and experienced woodsmen preach about dressing in layers. This is a wise bit of advice but where do they put the extra layers when they have to take them off? If they had an empty backpack they could put them there, and not have any extra weight than when they started the day. Before I used a pack, I would find myself keeping that extra shirt on, and working up a sweat as opposed to taking it off because it was inconvenient to carry while I tried to hunt. Ahhh, versatility, a beautiful thing. How many times have you become thirsty while hunting? With a backpack it is easy to carry enough water, and it's important to stay well hydrated, especially if your going to be putting on a lot of miles that day.

One of the neat things about being in the back country where other people don't frequently go is that you oftentimes find little treasures that you might like to bring home. A back pack is a convenient way to carry them without interrupting the hunt. I've carried out shed antlers in my pack as well as pounds of delicious wild mushrooms. I keep a plastic shopping bag in my pack in case I find mushrooms. It crumples up, stores nicely and weighs nothing. Without the advantage of a pack, carrying out eight pounds of wild mushrooms might be nearly impossible without canning the hunt for the day, so you might say a pack opens up opportunities.

Many times I leave my lunch in my truck because I don't like to carry anything I don't have to, but it's real easy to put it in my pack if I don't think I'm going to be near my truck at lunchtime. When dragging out a deer, I generally start to overheat, so the layers come off.

Ever try dragging a deer while carrying a gun and extra clothes? I know I have, and it doesn't work. Usually, you end up dragging the deer, and then going back to get gear, before dragging the deer again, better known as the leap frog method (inconvenient, many extra miles of walking). I've customized some light weight Velcro nylon straps onto my pack that will hold my gun, admittedly not a real convenient way to carry a rifle, but it works good enough while dragging. I stuff my extra clothes into the pack itself, and the chore of dragging a deer is made much easier. Did somebody say streamlined or agility? Oh baby! I guess my point is that carrying a backpack is not about carrying extra stuff, it's about versatility, opening up opportunity, and carrying the stuff you normally carry more efficiently.

Now, I'll list all of the stuff that I carry on a regular basis in my small, streamlined, virtually no weight pack. It's all of the smaller stuff that I've always carried while deer hunting. It fits neatly into the side pockets, and zippers of the pack, again the main compartment is almost always empty. I carry a small piece of trapping wire that serves a couple of different purposes. I stuff my tag in the deer's ear and wind the stiff wire around it. This sucks the ear closed, and I don't have to worry about the tag pulling off at any time during transport. You don't have to worry about poking a hole in the ear and making life tough for your taxidermist. The wire method is quick, easy, and effective. Besides, in case you haven't figured it out yet, my deer don't always have a giant set of antlers to put a tag on. This wire can also be used to attach a moose antler to the outside of my pack in case it is too big to fit inside.

Another item I carry is bright orange surveyor's tape. I usually will carry less than half a role as it is smaller and lighter in weight, and there is no need to have such a large amount of tape. The tape can be used to flag any found antlers that might be visible on your back for safety purposes. Unless I'm hunting on snow or I visibly see the animal go down, the first thing I do after shooting is pull out the orange tape, and mark the spot that I shot from. This can be invaluable while trying to figure out where the animal was standing when you shot, and sorting out blood trails.

It goes without saying, but a compass is a must. The compass is important enough that I actually carry two. One in my pocket for convenience of use, and another in my pack in case one should get lost or broken. A lighter or some other way to start a fire is a must. All stuff that is carried neatly in the side pockets. A drag rope and camera rounds out my list of carried things. The camera is the one extra thing that I can honestly say I wouldn't carry if I did not have the pack. However, I think this is a good thing. In the field, pictures when an animal is freshly killed and not gutted out, are much nicer than a picture of a gutted stiff deer in the back of a truck. I will mention that, obviously, I carry a knife of my own making, but this goes on my belt.

There you have it. Carry a backpack without carrying extra stuff, it will make you more versatile, agile, streamlined and open up opportunities.

While on the subject of gear, I'd like to talk briefly about hunting boots. Please do not skimp on your boots. Quality footgear is a must. I spent a week hunting, and camping in New York state, and rubbed a raw spot on my ankle from too much walking without the proper foot gear. Lack of showers, and lack of a good way to dry stuff out while camping led to an infection in my ankle, better known as blood poisoning. Being that I'm stubborn, or thick headed might better describe it, I continued hunting. I did get my deer, but, on the last evening I hunted, my ankle had ballooned to twice its normal size. I sat down to take a stand because it was useless to try and walk on it. The ankle and foot stiffened as I sat, and when I stood up to walk out as evening approached, I was shocked that the pain had become so severe when I put pressure on it that I couldn't walk on it. I arrived back at camp well after dark using my rifle as a cane, and hobbling around like a Hobbit.

We left the next morning and started the 12-hour ride home. When I arrived at 11:00 p.m. I was inclined to go to bed, but my wife had other ideas. She made me go directly to the emergency room as I had red lines streaking all of the way up to my knee, and my foot was swollen like a balloon, and beet red. After intravenous antibiotics, a prescription, and a good tongue lashing from the doctor, I was sent home with strict orders not to get out of bed for four days! It was tough to do, but the doctor figured amputation was the alternative, so I did heed his advice, and I'm quite happy to say I still have my leg. Sure would have been much easier to have had the proper foot gear. Seems like I'm constantly learning things the hard way.

What I will say, as far as hunting boots are concerned, is that waterproof is probably the single most important factor when choosing a boot. For years I wore just straight rubber boots. The olive-drab green, knee-high variety. Wet feet are cold, uncomfortable feet, and dry feet are warm toasty feet. You want something with good traction on the bottom, and insulation to suit your hunting conditions. David Haine turned me on to the Muckboot, which is for now my boot of choice. They are light weight waterproof, comfortable, and as warm a boot as I have owned. I have the model with the most insulation.

The last thing I will mention is long underwear. This is the layer that goes next to your skin. I recommend polypropylene. It is very warm and keeps you dry as it wicks moisture away from the skin. You can generally find this material at a reasonable cost. That wraps up all of the advice that I have as far as hunting gear is concerned.

> *For everything there is a season, and a time for every matter under heaven.*
>
> *Ecclesiastes 3:1*

16

AUTUMN SMOKE

I punched my 2006 deer tag, after the field dressing chores were done, there was nothing left of the deer season but the drag out. When I'm with someone else, they inevitably want to rush to get that deer out. If I stop to sit on a stump to relax awhile, they inevitably take over, yanking, and pulling the deer. An otherwise pleasant experience is turned into a back-breaking, lung-busting rush. The drag out is a lot of work no matter what, but it's one of my favorite parts of the hunt, especially when I'm alone. It's a time to reflect, and savor the experience, to bask in the feeling of accomplishment and success. Time is constantly a factor in the hustle and bustle of everyday life, but out here in the woods when dragging a deer, time means nothing.

On this particular drag, I was dragging up a steep hill, and I could only go 30 or 40 yards before stopping for a break. I even stopped for 15 or 20 minutes just to drink it in. Eventually I found the top of the hill and located my favorite tree — an old hemlock. I leaned up against its trunk which was roughly the size of a 55-gallon drum, and as I sat amongst the fallen leaves, the cool air felt nice, a great combination with a warm sun on my face. It was good hanging weather for meat. I sat there for a nice long while under that tree peering out through it's low sweeping evergreen branches. I had my musket by my side, and another New Hampshire deer just below me on the hillside in the leaves, and as I dozed on and off I reflected on the hunt, and basked in the feeling of satisfaction that comes with a successful hunt. It felt nice for once not to be in a rush to get somewhere. I certainly was in no rush to get back out to civilization — moments like this come far too seldom.

REFLECTIONS

Also while I sat leaning against that old hemlock, I found myself remembering hunts from the past. The muzzleloader season is my favorite season, and I've taken the majority of my whitetails with a muzzleloader. There's just something about the smell of burnt black powder on those frosty mornings that really speaks to my mountain-man-soul. It gets me longing for wild places, and the pursuit of deer in the swamps, bogs, and mountains of the New England autumn woods with the added challenge of a single shot muzzleloader, or musket as I like to refer to them. The first deer I took with a muzzle gun was taken with a .54 caliber hawken-style side lock with open sights that my father had given to me for Christmas. I killed that deer at the bottom of a mountain in a hemlock grove. It was a button buck that had approached from behind me as I sat leaned against a small hemlock tree. I heard the deer, and by the time I caught the movement out of the corner of my eye, it had already approached to within 10 yards. I could tell the deer was getting nervous, so I silently cocked the hammer. That deer sure enough was getting ready to bolt so I swung around, and snapped a shot off. Even as the deer reacted to the movement in a bound toward safety, my iron sights still found the shoulder. I didn't have time to think about it, and the shot was almost an instinctive action. It's a shot that I'm still proud of to this day. Granted it was only a button buck, but I was a teenager then, and this was only my second deer. This was a mountain deer, which are seldom easy to come by in any size, so it was a fitting place to cut my teeth with the "smoke pole."

I was uncertain of my shot at first, but once reloaded, I soon found red splattered amongst the colorful fall leaves on the forest floor, and my nostrils filled with the smell of the burnt black powder that still lingered in the air. There must have been something magical in that smoke, because I've been hooked on muzzleloaders ever since. I followed a heavy blood trail a short distance to my winter's meat in that hemlock grove, and then faced a long uphill drag. I wasn't smart enough then to kill a deer on top so that it would be a downhill drag, and apparently I haven't learned much since.

A doe taken with my side lock .54 caliber open sighted muzzleloader.

Another year that stands out is when I went to New York on a doe-only-black-powder-hunt. I got my first taste of traveling to hunt. I was amazed at how different deer hunting was just a nine-hour drive away. The wide-open spaces of the farm country were refreshing, and different than the claustrophobic big woods I was used to. I was also amazed at the amount of deer I was seeing on the roadside. Unfortunately there was a shortage of public hunting grounds, but after bribing a farmer with a woodcarving that I had made and brought with me, he was persuaded to let me hunt. The very next day the old smoke pole made meat again. I made my way through the corn in the early pitch-black morning. I remember the excitement, I felt as I settled into my blind in this far away place. I gazed up at the heavens that were full of stars with no trees to obscure the view. As a young hunter who was only used to seeing a handful of deer during an entire hunting season, the anticipation was almost unbearable to be hunting in a place so full of deer sign.

The dark slowly faded to early morning light, and again the deer approached from behind along a corn row. I slowly inched my way around, with my jaw locked tight, knowing at any moment this deer was going to spook. That deer had me contorted into a pretzel by the time my iron sights settled on to her shoulder and made the shot. She painted that whole front row of corn red before she crawled into a tangle so thick I literally had to crawl in on my hands, and knees to drag her out.

Later that very same fall, after returning to New Hampshire from New York, I took another doe on an evening hunt. I was hunting alone in between two bogs that created sort of a funnel. She was one of those squirrels that materialized into a deer. Judging by the noise she was making, I honestly thought she was a squirrel, but I propped my musket up in that direction just in case, and I was lucky I did. I think she had a nose full of me, because when she appeared from around the knoll she was stomping her feet, and bobbing her head. It didn't take long for me to let go with my iron sighted .54, and when I did, it knocked her flat right where she stood.

Another smoke-pole hunt, and another year found me seated beneath yet another hemlock tree, It was nearing 10:00 in the morning and the wind was picking up pretty good. I was getting ready to leave, but I was playing the "just a few more minutes" game when I noticed a deer walking along at a fairly steady gait. I noticed right away that it was a buck, but didn't pay much attention to that. I was concentrating on finding that shoulder in my .50 calibers peep sight. He was as close as he was going to get, so I let out a grunt with my voice to stop him. It worked, but as he stopped he immediately angled toward me. Despite the discouraging shot angle, I didn't hesitate because a moment's hesitation can mean the difference between success, and failure.

**My wife Alyssa posing with a small buck taken with an
open sighted .50 caliber side lock muzzleloader.**

The .50 caliber I was shooting is the most beautiful firearm I own. It was fitted with a piece of highly figured walnut before the Thompson center arms company's wood division burned. It's not front heavy like most side-lock muzzleloaders. It's short barrel handles more like my .30-.30, and it's narrow neck of a handgrip just lends nicely to the overall fine lines of the gun. The barrel has a high luster finish, and a rubber but plate completes the gun, insuring that she's gentle to the shooter. Don't let the beautiful curves fool you though, much like some women, despite the good looks, she's still wicked by nature as that poor five-point buck in my peep sight found out. The steady wind whisked away the gun smoke fairly quickly, and that deer's life drifted away from him in much the same manner. I could see by the way the deer reacted that he was hit. I found a small tuft of hair, and some bone chips mixed with tallow, but no blood trail. Despite the lack of blood, I found the deer just a stone's throw from the small knoll I had last seen him disappear over. The reason this muzzleloader kill stands out is that as I sat there in the leaves beside that deer giving thanks like I always do, it was the first time that I had done so with a ring on my finger — I had been married less than a month before.

TRICKS OF THE TRADE

Note: These are the tips and techniques that I use to be successful. They may not necessarily be safe. If you choose to use any of this advice, you do so at your own risk. Always read the firearm manufacturers instructions, and contact them with any questions or concerns.

I've taken a good many deer with an open sighted muzzleloader, but in recent years I've gone over to a scope, and I also have an inline that I use for foul weather hunts. The scope is good for low light conditions, as a good low power scope will gather light. The single most important piece of advice I can give you concerning muzzle loading, is to keep those muzzleloaders clean. These guns are not like your center fire rifle that shoots smokeless powder. Black powder, and pyrodex are very corrosive. If you let that gun sit overnight without cleaning it after you've shot it, you've done that gun an injustice. The metal will start to pit that quickly. If you let it sit a week without cleaning it, my opinion is that the gun is no good any longer — go get a new one. If you can't keep your gun clean, muzzle loading is not for you.

I've tried to give people this advice, but some just brush it off as me being anal. I watch people mistreat there muzzleloaders in this way, and then they complain about the "unreliability" of the muzzleloader when just the cap goes off, and the gun itself does not. The truth is that most of the time the nipple hole is probably sealed over with rust. If your gun is kept clean, and properly cared for, you will not have a misfire. In all of the hunting situations I've been in with a muzzleloader, I've never had a misfire. I've observed these same careless people complaining about accuracy problems the next year. I can't stress enough, it all comes down to keeping those muskets clean. If I have to look at one more rust encrusted muzzleloader being hauled out of the case for a day of hunting, I think I'm going to get sick.

A large doe taken with an in-line.

Some advice that I've learned about muzzle loading: If your shooting a gun with a #11 primer cap, after the gun is loaded, go ahead and unscrew the nipple and put a pinch of powder down the nipple hole and then re-insert the nipple. This is kind of like insurance. With the old side lock percussion cap muzzleloaders, the wrist section of a latex glove can be cut off, and then shimmied down the barrel to where the hammer is. Stretch it over the hammer so as to form a "tent" during foul weather hunting, and always keep your muzzle pointed down so rain water cannot enter the end of the barrel. The latex will flex with the hammer as you pull it back, and will not inhibit the gun in any way, and it will keep moisture out of the nipple area.

Again, I'll say that I've never had a misfire with a muzzleloader while hunting. If that gun doesn't go off for any reason, it's not the gun's fault, its yours. The modern in-lines are much easier as far as foul weather is concerned. They did a test where several in-lines were submerged completely under water, and then shot at different intervals. I want to say that most of them went in the neighborhood of a half hour before they wouldn't shoot. So help me, my gun will never get that wet. The last piece of advice I will give is to mark your ramrod so you can tell at a glance just by inserting the ramrod if the bullet is seated properly or even if the gun has a charge in it.

BACK TO THE STORY

Going back to the beginning of the story, you'll remember that I was sitting under a hemlock to rest while dragging out my 2006 deer. As I sat there under that hemlock tree on the hillside reflecting on hunts past, I figured it was time to drag some more, and my thoughts drifted back around to the present, and how I'd come to harvest the deer that lay before me in the leaves.

The 2006 New Hampshire deer hunting season started off with Dad, my grandfather, and myself camped out in a borrowed pop-up camper. We arrived the night before the muzzleloader opener, and would hunt the first three days of the season. The weather did not cooperate, it was a combination of heavy winds, and heavy downpours for the entire duration of our stay. Regardless, we hunted hard, and on the third morning my grandfather had a nice big doe within 50 yards, but the one time the sun decided to pop out for a half hour, it glared into his scope, and before he could sort out where the doe was through the glare, the deer winded him and bolted. We returned home three very soggy hunters with no venison to show for our hunt.

I hunted on my own for the next few days, and found an area with abundant deer sign. I set up at daybreak under a hemlock tree to overlook an area where deer had been crossing. About 45 minutes after settling in I caught a flicker of movement, and my heart raced a little. I thought for sure it was going to be a deer, but a coyote popped into view. Though coyotes are abundant in my area, it's somewhat rare to actually see one of these elusive animals. I made a deer grunt with my own voice, and the coyote stopped perfectly in a small opening. My gun was up on my knee, and I watched the coyote just over the top of my scope. When it stopped in the opening, I slipped the scope to my eye only to find it fogged. I quickly cleared the lenses with my fingers just enough to see through, but by the time I got on the coyote he was on the move again.

I shot at him as he trotted along, I instantly heard yipping, and as I peered under the plume of smoke, I saw the coyote biting at his side. I was surprised, and a little concerned as he proceeded to run out of sight. The .50 caliber slug should have knocked him flat if I had hit him solid. As I reloaded I was tempted to get up, and go look for him, but it was still early, and I still had hopes of seeing a deer.

About an hour after the coyote, I picked up on more movement, and as I watched, I made out at least two deer moving through the woods about 75 yards out. I picked up bits and pieces of a doe, and I probably could have shot, but I was holding off in hopes that they would come closer, and offer a more open shot. You only get one chance with the muzzleloader, so it has to count. Although the wind seemed to be in my favor, the deer's body language told me they were unsure of something. As they melted out of sight all together, I scolded myself for not taking the shot. A short time later I saw movement again right in the same area, and it was the same big-bodied doe. She wasn't any closer, but being blessed with a second opportunity, I decided I wasn't going to let it slip away from me again.

I finally found a small opening, and held on it. When the deer entered it, I found the shoulder, and let her go. I could see the doe through the haze of the muzzleloader's smoke as she barreled directly toward me. She covered the distance quickly, and appeared to be bounding 10 feet in the air. I was concerned about my shot as it had been through a small opening. I was thinking to myself as she came closer that if I had cold souls (my 30/06), she'd be in a heap of trouble, I could have emptied my gun.

A doe taken with my inline on a solo hunt out where the moss grows .

As she sailed across not 10 yards in front of me, I audibly said oops! I could see a bright red stain just behind her shoulder, and I knew she was in a heap of trouble anyway. On her second bound after getting by me she landed in a small clump of firs, and she didn't bound out. A small beech tree about the size of your wrist shook violently back and forth a few times and all was still.

I knew the doe was not going anywhere, so I went to look for the coyote. After plenty of searching, I wasn't able to find the coyote, so I returned to the doe, and the drag out that eventually lead to me sitting under the hemlock tree reliving hunts past.

That night with a belly full of fresh tenderloin, I carried an armload of firewood around the corner of my garage, the wood smoke from my wood stove carried by the chilly evening air filled my nostrils, and I was once again taken back to the hunt earlier in the day when my muzzleloader's smoke had done the same thing. I looked up, and the smoke from my chimney could be seen curling out against the dark of the sky, and the light from the hunter's full moon illuminated my winter's meat hanging from a tree across the yard. I stopped for a moment as the satisfaction hit me again, and also a twinge of sadness as I knew the fall ritual had been completed for another year.

The stuff dreams are made of. Dad and myself displaying our antlers at sunset in northern Quebec.

A Quebec Labrador caribou taken on the "Cold Souls" hunt.

My first caribou taken on the "Cold Souls" hunt. This animal was taken at 150 yards, notice the shot placement.

Three generations tag out on opening day in Maine. From left to right: the author, Bill Wilbur (grandfather), David Sargent (dad). There are a lot of people that will try and convince you that the only worthwhile hunts are the ones that involve huge trophy antlers. Some of my most memorable hunts involve taking deer without "big horns." This is coming from someone who has held a few sets of large antlers of various types in his hands. Again, I can honestly say that some of my most cherished hunts don't involve antlers. See the chapter entitled Bog Deer to read the story that goes with this picture.

A few furs trapped by the author.
Take notice of the stack of beaver pelts in my left hand.

A couple of coyotes trapped in the dirt.

Dad's Newfoundland caribou where it fell. Look at that smile, that's one excited hunter. One of the things that I have learned from dad is to find sign and stay with it. Many times I jump from area to area as I get bored with the same scenery, and think my chances are better if I keep moving. Dad finds sign, and keeps hunting the same sign relentlessly, and has had very good luck with this method. His reasoning is that he is eventually going to get an eyeball on the animal making the sign. This is the practice that enabled him to take this trophy woodland caribou.

Dad and I stand next to my first deer taken at age 13. This is where it all started for me, I was bitten by the hunting bug-hard. I don't know where the years have gone, but we have a lot of great memories to look back on and cherish that revolve around the outdoor experience. Thanks dad for taking me hunting.

The big stag I took in Newfoundland (Kill a Big Stag and Catch a Big Trout)

A big Buck killed by Lou Gagnon. What a classic looking picture. A big buck hanging from the rafters of a woodshed, and a Maine registered snow machine in the background. Even the wooden chair adds a little something that I can't quite find the words to describe. All of this by the light of a "gunmetal gray sky."

163

The author and his "Caribou Mountain High" antlers.

The bog buck and my "Cold Souls" rifle.

A tasty find of oyster mushrooms. I didn't kill a deer on this outing, but I still came home with something delicious to eat. Most mushrooms that grow in a shelf-like pattern on a tree are hard and nothing you would want to eat. This is one of the reasons the oyster mushroom is easily identified. Notice the gills on the bottom side of the mushrooms that radiate out.

Another edible mushroom that grows during hunting season. The sulphur shelf mushroom, or chicken of the woods is bright yellow and orange making it easily identifiable. Harvest when the mushroom is still young for best edibility.

The 40 foot tall Indian head that towers over the Author's woodshop (yes that's my woodshop under that giant snow drift).

A carving created by J.W. Sargent. Chainsaw carving taken to the next level with hand tools to create a greater level of detail.

17

LITTLE WHITE FEET

It started in the early morning darkness on the 20th of Oct. 2005. I left my truck, and with my little wooden bow proceeded into the blackness of the forest with hopes of reaching my public-land deer stand just as legal shooting light would arrive. It's a journey I've made dozens of times in the dark, but at this early date, the hardwoods still wore their brilliant foliage, and I was caught off guard as things looked much different. I soon found myself a little mixed up. After trying to right myself for quite some time, I finally gave up, sat down, and resigned myself to wait for daylight at which time, hopefully, I'd get my bearings back. At last, the eastern horizon began to glow with the days coming light. I proceeded in that direction, and soon found myself back in familiar territory, though quite behind schedule.

I arrived at my stand late, but I wasn't too hard on myself. This was my first trip of the year into the New Hampshire deer woods, and in 10 years of trying to take a deer with a bow, some years more intensely than others, I hadn't been successful. In fact I'd only had opportunity to shoot at one animal within bow range in all that time, which I missed. Being realistic I knew this trip was more of a scouting trip for the coming muzzleloader season as these New Hampshire big woods don't always give up their prize within bow range. Even more than scouting the area, it was an excuse to get out and drink in the beautiful New England foliage, whose colors my refreshingly light little wooden bow seemed to melt right into. An excuse to once again enter the crisp early morning air with nothing more than a stick, a string, and the ambition to battle against the odds no matter how insurmountable they may seem.

As I settled in, and knocked an arrow, it began to mist, and soon the woods were noisy with the drippings of the moisture laden leaves. That explains why I didn't hear her, but as I looked up she just came to me out of the mist like a gift. She was on a course that would take her not out of bow range, but within 23 yards. As I came to that realization, my heart really started pounding. At 28 yards she stopped behind some foliage that we couldn't see each other through, and as her legs began to move again I felt the feather fletching on my arrow brush against my lower lip telling me I had reached full anchor. As she stepped into the clear the thing that struck me most, as the arrow left the shelf of my bow, was the quiet, almost innocent sounding little shhhhthwump. I've always been accustomed to KA-BOOM!, when shooting at deer, but the forest went on with its natural rhythms as though nothing had happened, and I'm not sure even the doe knew anything was all that out of place as she trotted over the crest of the ridge after standing there for several moments out of bow range looking back in my direction.

I felt as though the arrow hit a little far back, and after replaying the shot in my head for about 10 minutes, I decided to climb down, and see if I could find the arrow. After reaching the soggy leaf-covered forest floor I stood there under the old hemlock a little chilled, I could see my breath as it bellowed out into the raw still air of the gray day, and just then my ears were filled with some of natures sweetest music. There was a good sized beaver bog about 150 yards away, and the ruckus those Canada geese made getting out of there told me something had spooked them. I made my way over to where the doe had been standing, and searched the disturbance in the leaves for any sign of a hit. I couldn't find any blood, but a small tuft of brown hair told the tale. I soon located the arrow, and confirmed what I had feared. The puke smelling green slime covering the arrow was very disappointing. My heart sank, and I felt my hopes start to diminish for retrieving my first bow shot deer.

Where the deer had stood before cresting the ridge, I finally located a blood trail. I was torn with what to do, but considering the wet conditions decided that I would follow the blood for as long as I could for fear that it would be washed away. The blood sign was getting very difficult, and sparse as I approached the beaver bog. In the direction the doe was headed there were large tangles of blowdowns, and my deer hunters instinct told me that she would surely be bedded amongst the mess somewhere. I decided to back off, and give her the recommended three hours for a poorly shot animal.

I sat under my stand for nearly three excruciating hours, and then with a glimmer of hope took up the trail again. Any signs of blood were gone, but I stayed on course in the general direction that she had been traveling. I searched beneath every tangle, and under every blow down. Several hours later I found myself back at the last sign of blood. The black of a crow could be seen standing out against the gray of the sky. He was resting atop a long slender gray log that was standing dead at the edge of the bog. I spooked him, and as he took off, I could hear the swoosh of his wings, and with a single caaaw!, he circled, and lit atop the very same branch.

The doe's course was following the heavy cover around the right-hand side of the bog, and that's where I had focused most of my attention, but perhaps she had circled back and to the left of it. Several more hours passed, and I had scoured the heavy edge cover all of the way around the bog. I walked in ever widening circles covering a great area, but I knew in my gut I wasn't going to find this deer. She wasn't in the thick cover where I was positive she'd be, and now I was out in the open hardwoods grasping at straws.

I've been shooting a traditional bow for three years. The previous seven were spent with a compound bow. One of the biggest differences that I've found in shooting traditional equipment is that the recurve is more of a commitment. With the compound, I could pick it up, and attain fairly reasonable accuracy within a week or two. The recurve requires daily practice throughout the course of the year which is a pleasure, not a chore. Shooting a traditional bow is a lot of fun. I love my recurve, and I'm fairly confident in my abilities with it. I like the simplicity of it, no sights or gadgetry, just look at what I want to hit, and let the string go. The fact that I'm depending more on my natural instincts to shoot, as opposed to sights, releases, and other technologies, it makes me feel like a true predator intertwined with the natural world around me. Early photographs of the Native Americans of old often show a wild look in their eyes, it's intriguing to know they, too, new the feeling of the string in their hands, as they set out into the wilds with the most basic of tools.

Considering my story so far, and the poor shot placement, I don't feel as though I'm in a position for giving shooting advice. There are certainly people more experienced, and better suited for this than myself, but what I'd like to do is give the beginner a starting point to build from. The two most important things for me, when shooting a traditional bow, are to focus intensely on a small spot on your target, and not to move your bow hand at all throughout the shot. Most archers already know about finding an anchor point. After this it's just a matter of lots of practice, practice, and more practice. You should practice so much that you no longer have to think about what you are doing, but rather it happens automatically. When you no longer have to consciously think about keeping your bow hand still, or being sure that you're anchored, then all you have to do is focus on the spot you want to hit. Start out shooting close to your target, and as you become more accurate, slowly increase your distance from the target. I'd recommend getting *The Traditional Bow Hunters Handbook* by T.J.

Conrads. It helped me a great deal, and will tell you everything you need to know from picking a bow, to setting up and tuning it.

A compound bow lets off 50 percent or more of its draw weight when pulled, allowing the archer to stay at full draw longer, which is an advantage, but shooting in the traditional style isn't all about disadvantages. When you shoot instinctively, you don't have to line up sights, which makes for a quicker style of shooting, and it's also better in low light conditions. The equipment is more basic, you don't have to worry about snapping off a sight pin, or any number of other things that can go wrong with gadgetry. True, it may be more challenging, but with greater challenge comes greater reward.

That being said, I'm not sure what happened with my shot on the doe, I guess the adrenaline factor came into play. People may say, yeah, but it's only a doe? For me it was an opportunity at a long awaited, and hard earned trophy. I've shot bigger deer with firearms, but I've been trying for years to connect with archery equipment. This doe was the diamond in the rough for me. I was feeling that success would have been too sweet if this hunt had come together, especially in my home state.

Getting back to where I left off with the hunt—the afternoon was wearing on, and I was convinced that as quiet as I had been, I must have spooked the doe when following up the blood trail, and that she was probably miles away by now. Once again, I found myself at the last sign of blood. I sat crouched there, soaked through, and dehydrated from walking all day, and not having anything to drink. It was noticeably darker in the damp thick of the spruce, and hemlock, as it was getting later in the day. I was feeling a bit lonesome and dejected, I looked up at the brighter sky, and noticed that my good friend the crow was still upon his perch. I was in disbelief that I had messed up an opportunity that I had waited so long for. Unfortunately stories like this don't always have a happy ending.

Nevertheless, I went back and thought once again through the whole shot sequence, only this time instead of focusing just on the shot, and the hit, I tried to remember everything that had happened. Suddenly It struck me about the geese spooking, a small but important detail that I had overlooked in the excitement and disappointment of the day. Maybe that doe had made her death run straight out into the bog, and spooked those geese. As I sat there in the woods, it sounded far fetched, but would also explain why the crow had stayed for so long.

Mother nature had been talking to me all day, but I just now had decided to listen. I wrestled my way out through the heavy edge cover, and into the wide-open bog, and my eyes just about popped out of my head with shock when I discovered my deer just 10 yards out into the swale grass near the edge of the water. As I had been crouched at the last sign of blood, I had been less than 40 yards from that deer, and had been considerably closer several times throughout the day. That deer was feeling sick, and I just wouldn't have guessed that she would have exposed herself out into the wide open as opposed to hiding in the comfort of the thick cover. On top of that there's no way that she would have crossed that bog, it just didn't seem a likely place for her to have gone.

After spending the better part of the day with a knot in my stomach, a wave of happiness poured over me as I sat there next to the doe in that bog. I was grateful to have secured my winter's meat so early in the season, and finally having a successful hunt with my recurve bow is such a thrill, and deep satisfaction that words cannot describe. I came to realize that she had actually had a fairly quick end, thinking back to the shot, it had only been about 10 minutes from when I let the arrow go to when the geese were spooked.

I soon noticed that she had what looked to be an unusual amount of white around all four of her feet. I didn't deserve this one, so I figured the white was leftover from making her way down through the clouds as surely she was a gift from above. On the drag out my legs began to severely cramp, from dehydration. As I sat there rolling around in pain on the ground at one point, I thought maybe this was my punishment for shooting poorly. After all, if I had made a better hit, the blood trail would have been easier, and I wouldn't have been in this predicament. I had learned once again to listen when nature talks (the geese, and the crow), not to give up too easily, and to search in even the most unlikely of places. These were valuable lessons that cannot only be applied in the deer woods, but also to life. I named my recurve bow "little white feet" so I would not forget these important lessons.

18

THE SQUALL

It was the last week of the New Hampshire deer season when I received a call from my dad asking If I felt like doing a little hunting, and did I have any ideas on where to go. After talking with my wife, she agreed to watch my woodshop for a day while I hunted with my father. I called dad back and told him I had a secret out-of-the-way spot that might be worth trying.

Being the end of the season, there were less deer to shoot at. The deer population can be sparse in the big woods areas we hunt, and the deer left at the end of the season are liable to be extra wary from being chased and shot at for a month. So I decided on hunting a remote spot that takes some walking to reach. It's exactly one and one half miles from where we park the truck to where we hunt. I had not hunted this area previously during the season, mostly because of its remoteness. I generally only get in there once or twice a year, and have never seen another hunter. My reasoning for choosing this spot was to get to an area where other hunters have not been, perhaps the deer would feel safe, and maybe the extra effort might pay off with a deer sighting. If we were really lucky, it might be a buck.

The alarm clock sounded, after pulling on my boots I headed for my truck. As I opened the door, the frigid predawn bite in the early December air instantly made me long for the warm bed I had just left, but there would be no changing my mind this morning as I knew my father was already en route to meet me.

The 20-minute drive in the early morning darkness was a quiet one — no other headlights at this hour in the morning. Opening day had been a different story with trucks scrambling to and fro. Most other hunters had either tagged out or given up. The quiet ride made me think of the solitude and remote quiet of the area we would be hunting, and I couldn't help but dream a little about the giant buck track I had seen in this area the two previous seasons, and wonder what his rack would look like, or if he was even still alive.

Soon we were at the parking area talking strategy. I told dad I was going to drop him off at the spot where I had killed my five-point buck the previous year. I wanted him to have the best spot as I already had killed a moose. I was one of the lucky few who had drawn a New Hampshire moose permit for the October hunt. Though we shared the moose hunt, I was the shooter, so I thought it only fair for him to have the choice spot.

Dad talked me into getting started in the darkness because it was a fairly bright night. The black star-filled sky was brilliant as I gazed up through the network of leafless branches while we crunched along through week-old snow. I lead the way through the darkness as I knew the lay of the land. The area is defined by a brook. The brook runs for approximately three miles before emptying into a large pond. Along its course it runs through several active beaver ponds, and through old, dried-up beaver meadows. It turns swampy in areas, and back to a narrow babbling brook in others. The flowage is bordered on both sides by very steep ridges, and in some cases even rock ledges. When you start down in, you feel as though your entering a remote canyon out west somewhere. It also makes for an extremely grueling drag as I had learned the previous year.

We dropped over the steep ridge and located the brook. I followed along the edge of a thick stand of alders and through one of those mucky, marshy areas that you would think would freeze up, but always seems to unfairly want to suck off your boots regardless of the cold. I always forget how long of a walk in it is. Dad had just asked, rather skeptically, if we were almost there. I think he was questioning my navigation abilities. To be perfectly honest, I was starting to question them myself, though I did not let on to him. The dark has a way of changing the way things look, letting doubt creep in, but when we reached several hemlock covered knolls, I knew we were almost at dad's spot.

I had him overlooking a beaver meadow with a deer crossing going through it. The grass that normally grew tall in the meadow appeared small, and matted down with frost. I nestled dad into a small bunch of jack firs with a rather large blow-downed log that glistened with frost along his side, perfect for resting his gun over should a shot present itself. He also had a tree to lean against, a cozy little hideout to say the least. I warned him not to focus all of his attention on the meadow, and not to be taken off guard if a deer approached from behind him as my five-point had done to me the previous year.

As I left him, the darkness was starting to give way to light, but still too early to shoot. My intentions were to walk until I found a likely looking spot, and sit for at least a couple of hours. I cleared the far end of dad's meadow and entered a thick stand of hemlocks. The flowage turned back to a babbling brook, and I followed it for a couple of hundred yards when I spotted what appeared to be an area where deer had been crossing as there were several sets of tracks in the week-old snow. I found a spot under a hemlock tree, cleared away the snow and sat down.

The bitter cold instantly started to gnaw at me as I had worked up a sweat on the way in. I had only been sitting for 10 minutes, when along with first shooting light, a small but somewhat intense snow squall arrived. As I sat bundled against the tree, I squinted against the pelting snow, and scanned through the hemlocks, when, across the brook, I could see the silhouette of a deer coming down off the ridge. I found the deer in my rifle scope which rested across my knees, and even though the deer was walking through brush, I could clearly see two long spikes protruding from his head, a legal buck. My heart raced, and I picked a spot between two trees where the deer would come into a small opening. I would only have a split second in which to shoot as the deer walked through. I was determined to get a shot off.

During muzzleloader season I had missed a chance at a couple of does due to hesitation in waiting for a better shot. As my scope filled up with the silhouette, I squeezed the trigger. At the crack of the rifle the deer bolted, and did not present a second shot. I gathered myself up, and as I made my way (some 80 yards) to where the deer had been, the snow squall turned off as quickly as it had started. I found the deer's tracks, and was sadly disappointed. It appeared as though I had foiled my last chance of the season. No blood sign, which should have been fairly obvious on the snow. As I followed the track further, my heart sank even more — 100 yards and still no sign of a hit.

I started back to my seat, beating myself up along the way. I don't get a lot of opportunities, so I feel as though I have to make good on the few I do get. As I sat there, I replayed the events in my head. The whole thing had happened so quickly. The snow squall, the deer, and the shot had probably only spanned a couple of minutes at best. It seemed like a dream, seeing the deer come out of the snow. If not for the tracks, I may have questioned whether it happened. About an hour and a half passed when dad finally came poking along, curious as to what I had shot. I, somewhat embarrassed, told him the story, and he double checked the deer's trail. He then proceeded to give me a little good natured ribbing about missing the shot. It was the first deer I had shot at and missed for several years. Feeling pretty dejected about ending my streak, I had dad sit in "the hot spot," and I headed off in search of greener pastures.

I still hunted for three more hours, and never cut another deer track. I circled back and picked up dad. We were both cold, and decided to call it a season. We would end this hunt like so many others, unsuccessful, but richer for the experience.

On the way out the little buck had been going in somewhat the same direction we were headed. The deer veered off up on the ridge, and the track cut back in front of us several hundred yards from where I had shot. My dad pointed out the track again. I looked at it thinking about what could have, and what should have been, when I had to double take. There was the tiniest speck of crimson red standing out against the white snow in the deer's track. Apparently the snow squall had been just enough to dust in and conceal what little sign of hair, or a hit where the deer had been standing at the time of the shot.

Astonished we began to track the deer which had returned to walking at this point. About every ten or fifteen yards there would be a small spot of blood. If not for the snow, it's doubtful the tiny specks of blood would even be noticeable. I figured the deer had been slightly nicked. Some time later the deer tracks started up the ridge to our right, which is uncharacteristic of a seriously wounded animal. As the deer went uphill, it seemed to chug out a little more blood which was encouraging. I was watching the track when my dad announced he had seen movement up ahead. I readied my rifle, and moved forward with my thumb on the safety. We came to where the deer had bedded, and a rather large puddle of blood, which was full of acorns. It was obviously a gut shot deer, but for the first time I really got my hopes up. The movement dad had just seen was the deer fleeing its bed. At this point, the deer was headed straight downhill, and the blood trail was very obvious. The deer entered a hemlock swamp. It had been approximately five hours since the shot. We followed through the swamp rifle at the ready, and as I crested a small hummock I spied the white belly of the dead deer resting under the bough of a low-lying hemlock branch.

Though I feel bad for the way the deer was hit, and even though it wasn't the big buck I had dreamed of, I would be lying if I said it wasn't one of the most memorable, and exciting hunts to have shared with my father simply because of the way it played out. We said a small prayer and gave thanks for the three-point buck. I set forth, happy to have someone with which to share the chores at hand. Though I felt bad that dad had not been the one to shoot, I was to be outdone by him in this very same area the following year, but that's another story.

> *The things you have learned and received and heard and seen in me, practice these things; and the God of peace shall be with you.*
> *~ Philippians 4:9*

19

KILL A BIG STAG AND CATCH A BIG TROUT

About 20 minutes after leaving the boat, and three quarters of a mile of hiking behind us dad suddenly blurted out "caribou!" Our attention was immediately riveted to the white spot, and, as our guide raised his binoculars, I could hear the excitement in his voice as he said "yeah, and it's a wicked stag, too!" I was caught off guard with surprise and excitement after mentally preparing myself for a long tough hunt. I never would have guessed my opportunity to come within 20 minutes of the first day.

Dad had shot first the previous year on the Cold Souls caribou hunt in northern Quebec, so this year was my turn, and I dropped to my butt, and extended the legs on my bipod in one fluid motion. I got on the caribou and squeezed one off. The shot felt good, but he didn't tip over, so I lined up on him again, and let loose. As good as dead I thought to myself, I was waiting for him to tip over, and decided to give him one more. I looked up at our guide after the third shot, and he said in an excited, almost scolding way, "take your time, take your time." That's when I began to realize I was missing.

A helpless confusion washed over me, I was screwing up what could be my only chance, and couldn't figure out why. After spending hours, and shooting thousands of rounds at the range over several years, I had an almost arrogant confidence in my shooting ability. In the excitement of the moment it never occurred to me that the animal could be out of range. I held a little high, and shot again. Our guide finally said come on let's get closer. In disbelief, I set off running to close the gap a little. I dipped down into an alder-choked stream that separated me from my prize, and all I could think of as I lost sight of the animal is that he might not be there when I came out on the other side.

This was Newfoundland not northern Quebec. Although we were here to hunt caribou, as we had previously in northern Quebec, there are several big differences. First of all, they call bull caribou stags, and second of all, there are not enough of them for me to have any business whatsoever of missing a shot at one. As a matter of fact, when we arrived on Sunday, our outfitter's brother dropped us off at a boat launch for the final leg of our journey to reach caribou camp, he wished us luck, and as he left told us it was going to be a tough hunt. I looked to the guide standing next to the boat who was left in our company and asked him what he meant by "tough hunt." That's when we learned that they had only killed three caribou in the last three weeks of hunting. I realized then that this would be similar to hunting deer back home in New Hampshire, every opportunity at an animal must be treated like gold.

The guide next to the boat was Danny, who was to be one of four guides in camp that week. He was a tall, solid man in his late thirties with a nose that leaned hard to the left. As he turned to load some gear into the boat, I observed a tattoo of a large bear track that covered the entire back of his neck. My first thought was that this guy is a hardcore hunter who loves what he's doing, and I wasn't far off. At the boat ramp with me were dad, my 74-year-old grandfather Bill, and a friend by the name of David Haine who has made a name for himself as a realtor in our hometown back in New Hampshire. The four of us loaded into the boat for the ride to camp.

Soon we were docked at camp, and unloaded our gear. On my previous caribou hunts in northern Quebec, we had stayed in plywood shacks with absolutely no electricity. That's what I was expecting, so you can realize my surprise when I stepped through the door, and heard Jimmy Hendrix crankin out of the radio, and somebody yelling to "rack em" from across the pool table. Now, 'I could get used to this" I thought to myself, flush toilets, and hot showers, and you could hardly hear the generator as it purred along in the shack out back. There's no hunting on Sundays in Newfoundland so the day was spent getting to know the other hunters in camp, and squaring away sleeping arrangements. Bernie, a police officer from New Jersey, was hunting for two weeks, and was starting his second week when we arrived. He had killed a small moose the previous week, and held tags for bear and caribou. In his week of hunting, he had not even seen a caribou. I thought if we were lucky somebody out of our group might get one.

That night we sat around the dining area and the guides felt us out as far as physical abilities, hunting styles and what not. There were four guides in camp, one for every two hunters. The guides would choose who they would be matched up with for the week, and the decisions would be announced in the morning over breakfast. Danny, and I both seemed to have dominant personalities, and clash a little, but I was secretly hoping that dad and myself would be paired with him. This is a guy who had spent a week out at sea the previous winter braving the arctic weather to kill baby seals off from ice flows by the hundreds for their pelts. To say he was a touch indelicate would be an understatement, but his rough demeanor suited me just fine. After surviving on little sleep, and having to be towed back to land by the coast guard, he still loved every minute of the seal hunt, and the money wasn't bad either. I had asked Gerald, a tall pencil thin guide in his sixties, when the best time of day was to see caribou. His reply was that there is no figuring out caribou. You're just as likely to see them at noon as you are in the morning. "They just seem to appear out of nowhere as if they had popped up out of the tundra itself."

Well the first morning of the hunt had arrived, and after a solid breakfast, Dad, Danny and I were found rocking to and fro as the boat's motor droned along through the first hint of the early morning's overcast of gunmetal gray. It was a cold six-mile boat ride. Paralleling the lake was a great ridge called Hinds Mountain, it's the type of ridge that makes you feel small.

When we ran out of lake, we continued to parallel the ridge on foot. Not ten minutes into the hike I spotted a cow moose about 150 yards off. We were hopeful that the animals would be moving as the weather had turned rather cool, or perhaps damp, and raw would better describe it. We were headed for a knob about a mile away that would allow us to survey the landscape for miles, including a huge portion of the ridge. After about another 10 minutes of hiking dad spotted the caribou, and that leads me to relieve the suspense of my opening paragraph.

As I fought my way out the other side of that alder-choked stream, I was relieved to see that the caribou, though undeservingly, was still there. Using a clump of spruce as a shield, I closed the distance to the 200-yard mark from what we later found out had started out to be 400 yards! I had managed to reload on the way, and when I dropped onto my butt again my next two shots found their mark, and the animal tipped over. The excitement of the moment was dampened slightly for me as I tried to overcome the embarrassment of my missed shots. I had been shooting under the animal, although one of the shots had hit the bottom knuckle destroying it's leg, which is probably why he didn't run. Caribou seem to just hobble around after they've been shot as apposed to running. The situation definitely served to take me down a few pegs, and a rangefinder will be a part of my gear from now on. I think Danny was more excited than either my father or myself, after three slow weeks he finally had a decent stag on the ground. He doesn't smoke, but a celebration was in order, and dad's cigarettes were the only thing handy, so smoke he did.

Dad and myself with a woodland caribou I killed in Newfoundland.

Here I sat not 30 minutes into a week long hunt with this beautiful mountain as a backdrop, and the chocolate colored antlers of a big stag caribou in my grasp, and my hunt over. We quartered and caped the animal, I hiked the antlers and cape back to the boat by myself, and then returned. At 50 pounds per quarter, dad and Danny each grabbed one, and I loaded two onto my pack frame. After dropping our load at the boat we hiked the mile back in and finished out the day glassing from atop the knob so that dad could have a shot. Short of a cow and calf, no more animals were spotted.

Carrying cape and antlers back to the boat after quartering up my animal.

The next morning found us in the same area. This morning we got all the way to the knob without spotting any caribou. It was a nasty wet morning, and the wind driven rain rendered my cheap binoculars useless more often than not. I decided to take a walk around the backside of the knob, and as I looked up, I saw a nice stag. He appeared out of the misty fog like a white maned apparition with his antlers thrown back, his head held high in the air, and on a flat out run. He was gone from view in seconds, what a lucky sighting. I ran to deliver the news to dad. Not long after that, Danny located some cows back in the direction of the lake. He had a hunch this is where the stag was headed, and his hunch proved right. We were soon stalking the group of caribou, and as we left the knob, we immediately lost sight of them, but Danny delivered us right up into there laps. We dropped down on the back side of an embankment. We were bent over at the waist, as we half ran half walked to get closer. There was a group of ptarmigan that nervously ran along beside us on the embankment. If they had flushed, it would have been game over as the caribou would have gone on alert. Dad finally crawled about 10 yards out in front of us, with his gun up as he waited, poised with patience for the stag to turn broadside. Danny and I were about to burst as the seconds dragged on with no gunfire.

Dad's woodland caribou. Notice the size of the bodies on these animals.

A fawn fed its way to within feet of dad, and Danny whispered that the fawn was going to blow the hunt for sure. About then dad's shot rang out, he had missed. The stag started to run, and he wasn't coming back. "Oh no," I said to myself as the disappointment hit me. I knew dad had time to shoot again, but in that split second I knew, a running ,follow-up shot isn't a high-percentage shot. When his second shot rang out, my disappointment turned to excitement. He had missed a standing still shot, and then rolled that old stag on the run. It's the best shot I've seen him make, and that caribou hit the ground as quick and hard as any animal I've ever seen. It's one of the most exciting hunts I've been on due to the build up during the stalk, and then the dramatic turn of events at the moment of truth. A father and son hunt that I will treasure for the rest of my days.

Dad's caribou had fallen close to a river that ran to the lake where the boat was. Danny suggested we float him out whole as apposed to packing him out on our backs. I wasn't going to argue with that, as a matter of fact it sounded downright appealing. It wasn't all peaches and cream though. Dragging the animal over some of the shallow areas was a lot of work, and I was wet to my waist with icy cold water by the time the back-wrenching job of dragging a 300-pound-plus, sopping-wet caribou into the boat was done. The thought of butchering that animal over a cup of hot coffee back at camp kept us going.

Dragging Dad's caribou down river to the boat whole.

The wind was blowing at a good clip, which made the boat ride back to camp a slow cold one. I shivered the whole way back, but as I glanced up at the rack protruding from the bow of the boat, I thought of the memories we had made, and a feeling of satisfaction warmed me from within. Danny smoked another cigarette and there was a feeling of excitement, and camaraderie in the air. Later that night we learned that David had also had a successful hunt.

I decided to hunt with my grandfather the next morning; his was the only tag left to fill. Gerald was his guide. We set out on an eight-wheeled Argo, which is like a mini tank.

The Argo all-terrain "tank" that we drove out through the Canadian bush on my grandfather's hunt.

We left being pelted in the face with rain, and it did not let up for the remainder of the day. The land was cloaked in a thick fog which made glassing any distance impossible. Gerald kept asking me where all the caribou were, apparently Danny had told him I was a caribou magnet. About eight miles out from camp, we finally spotted a group of four or five caribou. We got within one half mile of them and then approached on foot. I don't know if there was something in the water or what, but my grandfather missed his first shot. The caribou ran up over a hill, and we ran after him. When we crested the hill, he was standing broadside looking back, and Bill knocked him down. Bill had had knee surgeries, and Gerald said to him I thought you couldn't run? We arrived back at camp toward evening. We had only traveled a total of 16 miles, but it took all day as the argo slowly climbed through bogs, mud holes and up and over boulders.

From left to right: David Haine, Bill Wilbur, David Sargent, and J.W. Sargent.

The pressure was off, and it felt nice to have a leisurely morning around camp to try and figure out if I wanted to go bird hunting or fishing. I decided to save the bird hunting for the next day and spend a lazy day around camp eating too much and wetting a line. The lake contained brook trout and landlocked salmon. I fished my way down the shoreline, and managed to hook some tiny salmon all of eight inches. As I looked up, I saw a boat coming. It was Gerald, and he happened to see me along the shoreline. He pulled up, and offered me to troll to the opposite shore where he had to pick up some gas. As I jumped in the boat, I wasn't expecting much after those tiny salmon, but the next thing I knew, I had a heavy head shaking bow in the rod, and a sizeable swirl on the surface behind the boat.

As the fish drew nearer, Gerald and I saw it at the same time, a swirl of brilliant red, and large blue spots, I couldn't believe my eyes. Gerald shouted don't lose it! That's a nice fish! I had always wanted to catch a large wild brook trout, and it appeared my day had finally come. I didn't want to count my chickens yet though, I had lost a similar fish in northern Quebec a few years previous, and this fish was making impressive drag peeling runs to the bottom every time he got near the boat. We didn't have a net, but Gerald is an Atlantic salmon guide at other times of the year, and he expertly landed the fish by hand. Words can't describe the brilliant colors on that fish when it first came from the water. I was as excited about that trout as I was my caribou, what a bonus to an already great hunt.

Dad had killed a half dozen or so spruce grouse with a single shot 20 gauge the previous morning. I had brought along my recurve bow, and intended on hunting birds with it. Dad said he'd like to get some footage on his digital camera of me shooting a grouse with my bow. The camp cook remarked that Dad might also get some footage of a Sasquatch at the same time. Gerald had a good laugh at my weapon of choice as well. He'd never seen a bow without those little wheelie things, and didn't think that primitive stick and string lent itself very nicely to bird hunting, and well, maybe he was right, but with greater challenge comes greater reward.

My grandfather Bill brought along a 12 gauge over and under, and Gerald said that I should shoot first, and when I missed Bill would follow up with the gun. The first bird we encountered turned out just as Gerald had predicted. We happened upon a grouse sitting in the dirt two track, my arrow sailed harmlessly just over its back, and as it flushed, the roar of Bill's shotgun cleaned the bird out of the air slightly before it reached the safety of the spruce trees. He'd made a very nice wing shot.

The next bird we happened upon was resting on a branch about 10 feet off the ground, I drew back, and the arrow caught the bird squarely, Gerald let out a whoa! As the bird flopped toward the forest floor, and a plume of feathers drifted on the morning breeze. The bird ran a little ways though, and after some looking, I caught him peeking from beneath a moss-covered log. I told Bill to bring me the shotgun as I had left my arrows out on the two track. I sighted down on the grouse, and shot, but only a click resulted. I switched barrels, and leveled on the birds head again, and shot with the same results. I handed the gun back to Bill. As he began to dig in his pockets for some shells, I walked up to the bird, and scooped him from beneath his hideout with my bare hands. Now, I could say I got the bird with my bow. When I brought the bird to the cook, I told her the Sasquatch had scared it into the tree, and I had shot it out.

Hunting for grouse in Newfoundland with my recurve bow.

Toward the end of the hunt, I pulled on my rubber boots, strung up my bow, and was out of camp at first light. I managed to take one more grouse with my bow on this early morning as I hunted alone along a river. It was a crisp clear morning, and the low angle of the early morning sun made the fall colors glow. It was picture perfect. As steam rose from the river, a grouse exploded from beneath my feet, and lit in a tree less than ten yards away. With my startled heart still hammering, I drew back with bare fingers as I had forgotten my shooting glove. The bird hardly fluttered as it fell to the forest floor. The bow string had been as sharp on my fingers as the air was on my face. I sat on a rock near the river's edge for a long time and reflected on the last few days. What a great hunt I had been able to share with my dad and grandfather. The older I get, the fewer and further in between those moments of perfect peace and tranquility seem to come, but as I sat there next to that river, all was right with the world. Life's kind of like that mountainous mixture of tundra and bush in Newfoundland. It can be very scenic and beautiful at times, but she can also be one rough ol'bitch.

Dad and I with our antlers, and probably more importantly, some of our meat hanging in the meat shed behind us.

20

BOG DEER

When I was single, and in my early twenties, I pulled up to a duck marsh in my little three-cylinder Subaru car. I jumped out with my 12 gauge, and set off to walk a piece of high ground that ran through the middle of a bog, and hoped to get a crack at ducks that often frequented the many puddles, and wet spots in the marsh. It wasn't long before there was an explosion from practically beneath my feet that set my heart to hammering, but instead of the whirring of wings, and feathers that I'd expected, brown fur, and gnarly horns materialized from the marsh grass.

I stood there with my jaw agape in disbelief as a tall racked whitetail buck charged through the grass, and down into a wet slough where 20 yards away he got bogged down momentarily. I watched the power in his back as his hind legs pump, and charge through the chest deep muddy water with very little progress, and that wild rack bobbed high above the whole spectacle. Finally he caught traction, and up into the grass he went. I thought of my bow sitting uselessly in the back of my car, and what might have happened if I'd only brought it instead of the shotgun. What was this deer, and a beautiful buck at that, doing in the middle of this duck marsh? Surely it must have been a fluke. Deer prefer the thick woods to a seemingly wide open marsh, don't they?

Fast forward ten years — I meet David Haine on a hunting trip as he was invited by my grandfather. David is a local realtor who lives, and works not far from my woodshop in New Hampshire. He also loves to hunt. When I first heard that David Haine the "realtor" would be joining us on a hunting trip by invitation of my grandfather, I thought to myself, "oh great, I'm going to have to deal with some yuppie type whose nose is so far up in the air that he's looking down his nose at everybody else." Boy, was I wrong. David is a hometown guy that came from nothing, and built a successful business, but you'd never know it to talk to him as he is very humble. One of the reasons his business has been so successful is because he grew up in the area, and knows the land better than most. Imagine my surprise when I started learning things about the outdoors from him.

David told stories of hunting wide-open bogs, and duck marshes quite successfully for deer. As a matter of fact he has a name for it. He calls it bog walking, and it's usually tough walking. It's something that other people rarely do, because your often walking on floating ground through knee-high vegetation that constantly wants to throw you off balance. The possibility of getting wet is very real. Oftentimes he'll bring a canoe, and cross a small piece of water, and then he is by himself hunting deer that have not been pressured. He told me that oftentimes deer pop up 50 yards away, and stand there and look at you, or they may pop up 150 yards away on a dead run. He's made many a running shot in the wide-open expanse of the bog. Any good Yankee hunter learns to make running shots as chances are often fleeting in thick timber. David says one of the advantages of the bog is that many times he improves as his gun begins to empty, and he realizes that he doesn't have many shots left, a luxury you don't have in the claustrophobic woods. He claimed that the deer actually live in the marsh, and they are not there because they have been pressured. I still had my doubts, about hunting deer in the wide open. I also had my doubts about how good of a deer habitat a bog is. That very year David killed his deer in the bog just like he said he would.

The following year after meeting David, I planned an early season bow hunt/camping trip with a good friend, Gary Larson, on the back side of several large bogs. We had to canoe roughly a mile by river into a wilderness area where we pitched a tent and hunted for a few days. We had no cook stove, but instead cooked our food over the open flame produced from whatever firewood we collected. We warmed ourselves next to the same fire in the early morning darkness before the hunt. There's something truly intriguing about using a fire as a practical necessity, and not just the luxury that most campfires are in modern times. It's a connection to the past, and to the native people that depended on the fire in a similar way. There's nothing better than sitting next to the crackling warm glow of a campfire with the smell of the wood smoke wafting through the chilly air, mixed with the smell of the inky black river flowing a few yards away, which was our only means of transportation. All of this beneath a black sky so full of stars that the mind can't fathom. Top that off with the anticipation of a recurve bow hunt in the morning, and you have a recipe for heaven on earth.

We both saw deer, but neither of us loosed an arrow on that camping trip. We gained plenty of knowledge for next year, and I was becoming more convinced, based on the deer sign, that David was right about those deer living in the marsh. I had to go back to work for a few weeks until rifle season opened, but I vowed to get one of those bog deer before hunting season was all said and done.

About a week before the rifle season was to open, David drove me around to some of his favorite bog hunting areas. Some of these bogs were wide-open expanses that stretched for miles. It was a different experience, and the idea of deer hunting in such a different wide-open terrain was kind of refreshing. I've gleaned bits of knowledge about the outdoors from different people, and learned plenty on my own, but I can say I've learned as much from David as I have from any other single person. I've nicked-named him "The Bog Father."

As we were leaving the bog on that day of scouting, David showed me another one of the bogs secret treasures. Nature's secrets seldom come easily, and I've been around many, many outdoorsmen, but this is the first time anyone had shown me the "hen of the woods." On the trunk of one massive old maple tree, too big for a half dozen men to stand hand-in-hand, and reach around, grew a mushroom of rather large proportions. The tree was old and twisted, almost grotesque looking, but all David did was keep chuckling with an occasional "oh my" mixed in, and more chuckling. He saw a thing of beauty.

The hen of the woods is a hard to find mushroom that is one of the finest delicacies to be had. It has an earthy and subtle nutty flavor. Little did I know that within a few days I'd be savoring that mushroom with fresh bog deer venison tenderloin. A treat that comes so seldom it must be relished. I felt like I was eating fancier than any king, and my meal could not be bought in any restaurant at any price. The bog gives up immeasurable treasure's to those who know where to observe such things, and David helped me to observe, and not just look — for that I am thankful.

After all of that scouting, the opening day of the Maine deer hunt finally arrived, and first light found us in a small wooded piece at the convergence of a river and pond with bogs for miles around. David and I talked before it was light enough to start hunting, and he asked me if I wanted to hunt down along the edge of the water by the river and pond, or did I want to take the high ground? I told him that this was his hunt, and his area, and I'd hunt wherever he put me. He started to talk, and then hesitated, and finally said "why don't you go down by the water." He knew the area well, and had hunted here many times. He wanted to hunt down by the water, and I didn't know it at the time, but he gave me the good spot. Something else that I learned later was that he always likes to hunt along the edge of open water when he can. The deer sign was good, "pretty fancy looking stuff" as David would say. We still hunted painstakingly slow. I could see David about 150 yards to my right.

Suddenly there were a few glimpses of deer up ahead going down towards the water. I put my rifle up to see if I could get them in my scope, but could not. Then I really slowed down, I knew those deer would be between me and the water, and they likely weren't going to cross that open water unless someone gave them reason to. It was an exciting hunt, because I knew they were right there. About 20 minutes later, I had lost sight of David, but I caught some movement about 70 yards away, and up on a knoll. It was the deer. I put my scope on a nice big doe, and with one well-placed, off-hand shot, my cold soul's aught-six flattened her. My dad and grandfather both killed a deer out of that piece before the morning was over. Three generations had killed deer in one morning, something that has never happened before. Ironically David didn't get his deer that morning, but about a week later he made another nice running shot in the wide open of — you guessed it — a bog.

The four of us hunted across three different states that year, and before the year was over, David had taught me how to find oyster mushrooms. Though not quite as rare as the hen of the woods, Oyster mushrooms are still not what I would call plentiful, but very tasty indeed. Another of natures treasures. I've been an outdoorsman for a fair number of years now, I've hunted trapped, and traveled to hunt, I've spent a lot of time learning about nature, and the animals, and how they interact with each other, and the land that they live on. I foolishly thought that I had learned the majority of what there is to know, and would occasionally find small tidbits of useful information, and was working on polishing my craft as opposed to learning. So to learn this much, and from a single source, is not only humbling, but something to be thankful for. I am finally convinced about those bog deer, and cringe to think of some of the places I've passed over as not being good deer habitat. I'm hooked on bog deer.

The results of bog hunting. Lou Gagnon and Jonathan Rhoades are pictured here with a 200-plus pound buck that Lou shot in a cranberry bog. Lou ran up to the buck after shooting it, and was pretty excited about the size of the animal. In his excitement he ignored the fact that the buck was not yet completely expired. The buck jumped up, and hit him in the chest with it's antlers. "Rookie mistake," Lou said laughing.

> *...see if I will not open the windows of heaven for you and pour down for you an overflowing blessing.*
>
> *~ Malachi 3:10*

21

THE BOG BUCK

When I turned 30 years old, I asked the good Lord that my family be safe, and well taken care of most of all, but if I were allowed any sort of a frivolous birthday wish for having to turn 30, maybe I could be allowed a nice buck this year. I had filled New Hampshire and Maine tags, and now we were hunting deer in another state, about a nine-hour ride from home.

It was getting late in the season, and I was running out of time for that wall hanger. Of all the hunts that we've been on, this is the first one that we were unlucky enough to get an outfitter that was less than desirable. It was Thanksgiving week, and being that we were 20 minutes from the Canadian border, this meant the weather was cold. Not only was the weather cold, but it proved to be downright hostile for the entire week. The first morning's hunt was clear, but with howling winds, and a temperature of 10 degrees it was downright frigid.

Generally we'd get up and walk in conditions like that to stay warm, but being that we were with an outfitter, we were on leased land, and were given strict orders by the outfitter, who we'll call Tom, not to budge from our tree stands. I was determined to give this guy the benefit of the doubt, and had no choice but to believe that he had our best interests in mind. So despite the outfitters general lack of respect for the people around him, and his surly demeanor, I respected his wishes, sat in that tree, and froze like a Popsicle. Despite the rough conditions, all of us hunted hard for the entire time, even my 75-year-old grandfather. The weather raged over the course of the week. It went from soaking rain to freezing rain, and about two inches of sleet, and then, finally, snow.

Tom had most of us situated on the edge of green fields, and my hunters instinct told me that this was a mistake this late in the season, but I continued to heed Tom's advice. The season had been open for six weeks, and I figured if I was a deer and had been shot at for six weeks, I'd probably not show myself in a green field. There was one stand that had produced a doe for one of our hunter's, and it was in the timber, other than that, no one was seeing any deer to speak of.

About midway through the week the hunter with the lucky stand killed another doe. After another hunter had an unsuccessful chance at the stand, I took a turn. Tom walked David Haine and myself into the stand in the early morning darkness. It was already cold and sleeting. On the way in, we had to cross a beaver dam, and my flashlight's beam had the pleasure of watching the rude outfitter, plagued so horribly with "little man's disease," slip and go face first into the icy knee-deep mud water. The "f" words were a normal part of his every day venomous conversation, but you've never heard such a string of obscenities in your life as he let go as he came out of that beaver dam's icy water.

I was going to ask him if he was all right, but I was having all I could do to stifle the laughter, and that would have just added insult to injury. He looked like a drowned rat as he headed back for his truck, and moments later we heard the engine of his truck roar to life. Thankfully nobody would be on the road at this hour as he had already displayed several fits of road rage, and in his condition it would have probably only been worse. David and I were left to find the stand ourselves in the dark. I climbed into the stand, and David went a couple hundred yards to my left.

As it began to get light, the sleet really started to come down. It was like little tiny pieces of birdshot, but made out of ice instead of lead. It began to pile up and coat everything. I made sure my scope stayed clear, but an inch of the frozen pellets lay frozen on top of the entire length of my rifle. About 8:30 I was really starting to get cold, the warmth of my hands had melted some of the sleet, and caused my hands to get wet, and so now they were cold, I was just thinking that I'd only have to endure about another half hour when a doe caught my attention off to my right. It was the first deer I'd seen, and I slowly started to pull my gloves off. My hands were cold before, but now, being directly exposed to the elements, were so numb, that I was having trouble making my thumb work to throw the safety off.

The doe seemed really jumpy and very cautious. She'd put her head down to eat, and then snap it back up to try and catch some movement. I think she was jumpy because of the other hunters that had frequented the stand who had killed deer in the last few days, and now she was on alert. Every time she'd put her head down, or her head would go behind a tree, I'd inch my rifle a little closer to my shoulder. Finally, I was looking through my crosshairs with the safety off, and as soon as the crosshairs touched her shoulder, cold souls roared. Lucky for me she only took a couple of steps, and then fell over dead, because when I chambered another round I couldn't get my bolt to close, due to the freezing conditions, and the build up of sleet.

It was a pretty scene laid out there in front of me. It seemed to be a world of black, and white with sleet covering everything, and weighing down the branches, but brilliant red jumped out of the white back drop framing the doe that lay below. I sat there, and gave thanks, and it wasn't long before David came poking along to see what I'd shot.

That evening we were all dropped off at tree stands on field edges again. There were five of us, and we had each hunted at least two stands. We began to realize now that there was snow on the ground that there was no deer sign around the stands anywhere. It became evident that Tom didn't have our best interests at heart. Whenever we tried to talk strategy with him, he basically, in a roundabout way, would tell us to sit in your tree stand and shut up. When we told him there was no deer sign around our stands, he went into a tirade about how much money he spends on leases, and these, "F-ing out of staters" tell him there's no deer in them, and that he'd have a mind to kick anyone off his properties who said such "b.s." It was beginning to become apparent that Tom just wanted to collect our money and dump us in a stand all week, to deal with us as little as possible, knowing full well that seeing a deer on these field edges, at this time of the year, was unlikely. There was no reasoning with this man, and the following morning was Friday, our last day to hunt.

Tom dropped me off at my tree stand before light on Friday morning. However. I didn't get in my tree stand. We'd all paid good money to be on this hunt, and had entrusted Tom to provide us with a good hunt. When the snow flew, and he didn't even scout out for fresh deer sign for his hunters, but instead dropped them off at the same unproductive stands, I decided I was going to hunt the way that I wanted to hunt despite Tom's dire warnings that we not walk his leases.

I spent the morning heading as deep into the timber as I thought I could get. It was the first time I felt like I had truly got to hunt all week, and what an enjoyable morning it was. Sneaking along on the fresh snow, I saw a fisher, and watched a pleated woodpecker for about 20 minutes, and wouldn't you know it, I began to get into some fresh deer sign, and boy I want to tell you when I found it, there was plenty of it. If Tom had done a little scouting, I think every man in camp would have taken a deer. I slowed down and hunted at a snail's pace like I do when I know there could be a deer any second. Take a few steps, and just stop and watch. Sure enough, I spotted a buck running a doe about 80 yards out. They blew through so quickly I couldn't get on them, but I knew where I would be for that evening for the final hunt. When I got up to where the deer had been, and followed their tracks, they had disappeared into a bog. I started out for the road because I wanted to be there in time for when Tom picked us up. I met David on the way out. He had apparently gotten restless as well. We hatched a plan to hunt that bog for the evening and final hunt.

There would be no sitting around the dining table talking strategy while sipping coffee, as Tom had put a lid on that at the beginning of the week with a tongue lashing about not coming to the dining hall until the dinner bell had been rung, and promptly started locking the door thereafter. So we secretly talked strategy back at the cabin, it was finally starting to feel like hunting camp with a little camaraderie, and strategy planning. Unfortunately, it was the end of the week, but we were determined to salvage one good hunt. At lunch time we asked Tom if we could be dropped off at our stands as early as possible, and he was all too happy to get rid of us — I mean, "accommodate" us.

Three of us jumped out of the truck and headed for the bog. We split up upon reaching the bog, and agreed where we should meet at dusk. I headed to where I had seen the buck running the doe. About 40 yards from the edge of the bog, I cleared the snow away from the base of a large hemlock tree, that seemed to have the best vantage point, and decided I was going to sit tight for a few hours. There were deer tracks peppering the ground everywhere, and considering it had been snowing when I started the morning's hunt, I knew the sign was smoking fresh. I don't mind sitting when the sign is that abundant. It was getting to be about two p.m. when I really started to get chilly. I took off my hunting hat, and slipped on a handmade wool hat that Cindy had made for me up in Labrador. I didn't know it at the time, but slipping that hat on when I did made for a new lucky hat. The cold was urging me to get up, and do some sneaking through the bog, but I wanted to stick it out as long as possible. I remember thinking how beautiful it seemed in that hemlock grove. It was really cold and snowing. Not a real heavy snow, but a spaced-out but steady snow. The overcast conditions with the large flakes of snow floating down out of the heavens, combined with the fact that I was in the softwoods, told me that the lighting should have been a little more dank or dim. The light however seemed bright, almost like artificial light, and everything seemed very crisp, maybe due to the cold. I remember thinking, "wow this is surreal."

I had a spot that I could see out across a section of bog, and into a small window on a ridge on the other side. It was probably only a six-foot window, but it was one of those spots that constantly caught my eye because it was a perfectly clear window that I could watch a section of ridge so far away while everything else around it was too thick to see through. It was one of those spots that you think you should see a deer there, but never do. Well, I happened to glance at it, and guess what? If I had happened to look even a second later, I would have missed it, but through that steady snow in that surreal light, I saw the perfectly crisp image of a beautiful buck walk through that six-foot opening. I grunted with my voice, and jerked my gun up hoping to stop him in the opening, but he was gone before I got the scope to my eye. I remember thinking, wow! "That's an image I'll never forget." I also felt a twinge of disappointment while I instinctively groped around in my pocket for my grunt tube. I knew that buck's course was taking him further away from me, and there was one gnarly stretch of bog between me and him.

I've never had a really favorable response to the grunt tube, but my thinking was that there was nothing to lose. I blew on that grunt four times, and wouldn't you know it, I started to hear what sounded like branches breaking near where the buck had disappeared, and soon it was unmistakable, there was a deer coming straight for me through that bog. As I watched over the top of my scope, I saw his antlers first — bobbing above the marsh grass. I had a flashback to the buck that I had kicked out of the marsh grass while duck hunting so many years ago as it was a very similar image.

I told myself not to get hasty, and shoot too soon, he was coming straight for me like he was on a mission. He popped up on my side of the bog, and I was watching him through my crosshairs now, but he was in a hollow where I couldn't see him that well through the brush. Then I saw him shake his head as he hooked some brush with his horns. He finally popped up in the wide-open 35 yards away on a small knoll. He was quartering to me, and turned his head sideways as he stopped on top of the knoll as if to look around for the source of the grunting. That shot angle was good enough for me, and cold souls flattened him with the first shot, but he promptly jumped up and began to struggle across in front of me. He came across close enough that I could see the wild look, and panic in his eyes as he passed, and he was noticeably struggling, as he battled to keep his feet.

The bog buck and my Cold Souls rifle.

The first shot would have done the deed, but I had instinctively chambered another round as soon as the first one left the barrel, and I drilled him again on his way by. He didn't fall that time, but turned back toward the safety, and sanctuary of his beloved bog. Only thing was, he fell about three feet short of the marsh grass. I walked up and admired my trophy, he was the best buck that I've killed. His eight point rack was fairly thick, symmetrical and tall. I felt very excited, with a sense of accomplishment. I'd spent a long time looking for a buck like this, I sat for a long while, and admired him. I thanked God for such a magnificent birthday present.

I still had one more doe tag in my pocket, so after dressing the buck, and dragging him back to where I was to meet the other guys, I went back to my lucky spot. I wasn't there a half hour when I could hear deer walking but just couldn't see them. As I scanned around trying to locate them, I caught them out of the corner of my eye walking behind me. The wind was blowing in a steady direction, and as soon as they stepped into my scent stream they held up with their noses in the air, but strangely enough they were looking in the other direction for the danger. That gave me time to settle my crosshairs behind the lead doe's shoulder, and seal the deal on my fifth deer of the year.

When the doe was dressed, and dragged up to where my buck was, I went ahead and dragged the doe the rest of the way out to the road. When I got back down to where the buck was I sat nearby and waited because it was getting late in the day at this point. I knew the other hunters would be coming out soon. I watched as three more does meandered by me, but did not shoot as I didn't have any tags left.

If Tom had done a little homework, we would all have had a successful hunt. I feel like we paid him good money and he failed us, so therefore, I don't feel bad about breaking his rules, leaving my tree stand, and making my hunt a successful one. We had paid him to hunt his property, and going against his rules was not illegal. What I do feel bad about is that we didn't catch on to him earlier in the week.

Hunting hard, day after day, in lousy weather can be hard enough, but a lousy outfitter really adds to the frustration, You know how the saying goes, the sweet isn't so sweet without the bitter. The bog buck is another memory I will cherish for the rest of my days.

> *"Every now and again take a look at something not made with hands — a mountain, a star, the turn of a stream. There will come to you wisdom, and patience, and solace and, above all, the assurance that you are not alone in the world"*
>
> *~ Sydney Lovett*

22

THE LOOSE SCREWS BUCK

The 2008 season started off to be a slow one. The previous winter had been brutal. In order to let light in, tunnels had to be dug down through the snow to my windows at the wood shop. The deer herd had been significantly reduced, a clear toll that the severe winter had taken. The opening day of archery season found me sitting in a stand that had a fair amount of good deer sign under it, as it always had. I couldn't quite figure out why I had never seen a deer here. With sign like that it would seemingly just be a matter of time. Despite the lack of deer sightings, this stand is one of my favorite places to watch the sun rise. It's a

211

place where the mountaintops tower over the treetops. During the gun hunt, when the leaves are down, the view is even more spectacular. Depending on the brilliance of the foliage, and the mood of Mt. Chocorua, the mountainsides ignite into a theatre of purple right on through to glowing orange as the sun's first rays reach deep into the White Mountain National Forest, and light up the east facing cliffs, and steep mountainsides. It's the sort of place that makes you feel very small. What a backdrop for a hunt.

As I sat there taking it in, I noticed some movement out of the corner of my eye. My heart rate instantly picked up as I was sure at first glance it was a deer. As it moved through the trees, I realized it was a red phase coyote. It was coming along at a quick enough trot that I had to grunt at it with my voice to stop it in my shooting lane as that would be my only opportunity. When I grunted, I was at full draw with my recurve bow, and the coyote did stop, but it zeroed in on me instantly. I let the arrow go, and as the coyote whirled to run I saw it stumble, and I did a little victory dance in my head.

I sat there for another hour before I went to look for the coyote as I was still really hoping the mountain would smile upon me favorably, and allow me a chance at a deer. After all, if I was fooling coyotes I surely had to be fooling deer, but none showed. When I got down, and went over to retrieve my arrow I was shocked at the lack of blood on the arrow shaft. There was a big clump of coyote hair there, however, no blood on the arrow tells the story. I just sat there in disbelief, trying to figure out what had happened. I had seen the coyote stumble. Considering that the coyote had been staring directly at me I think he had jumped the string like a whitetail does. As he crouched to jump, the arrow sailed over his back giving him a haircut, and throwing him off balance, hence the stumble. That was one lucky coyote.

I didn't know it at the time, but that was the most excitement I would have for the entire bow season. I never saw a single deer in the woods during bow season. There was a build up of excitement in anticipation for the first week of gun hunting in Maine. Not only did I not get a deer in Maine, but I never even got to see one during the first week. One of the hunters in our group that had a doe tag got a nice doe, but other than that it was track soup. That harsh winter had definitely taken its toll on the deer herd.

The muzzleloader season in New Hampshire finally opened, and this is my favorite season. I hunted hard the first couple of days without seeing any deer, and then the decision was made to get back to working full time, and hunting part time instead of the other way around. Toward the end of the muzzleloader hunt, I decided I would hunt for a couple of hours after work out of the stand I had missed the coyote from at the start of the archery season. It had been several weeks since I had been in there, and I figured it would be worth a shot. As I jumped out of my truck eager to get going, the realization that my green tote containing my hunting gear was not in the back of the truck struck me like a load of bricks. I almost called it a day right then and there, but I did have my muzzleloader and the single shot that it contained. I found an ignition cap down by my shifter, and I was back in business.

It had been very brisk in recent weeks as hunting season generally is, but the day had been unseasonably warm. All I had was the work clothes I was dressed in, and if it had been a day before or after, I wouldn't have been able to sit still on stand for 10 minutes without freezing. Maybe my luck was changing, after all some of the best hunting and fishing trips start off this way — I tried to convince myself. Sometimes things seem to come together in my life as if I were on a predetermined road map. I felt naked as I made my way into my stand without all of the camo and gear that I generally hunt with. I noticed a smoking fresh scrape within sight of my stand, and that made me feel pretty good. I looked at the track in the scrape, and I said, "Yep, I'll take that one, Lord." Be careful what you ask for because you just might get it — I'll explain later.

Most of the hunt was spent enjoying the view, and watching the blue jays, and other small forest animals. It was getting along toward dark, and I was almost ready to get down when I heard something approaching, and could see bits of movement through the trees. I had no idea what it was or if it would even come in my direction, but pretty soon I heard it step into the water, and as it sloshed along I knew it was inevitable that it would step into view pretty soon.

213

The deer appeared to be a little better than knee deep as it sloshed along through the small bog in front of me. It took a little looking through the scope, but I was convinced that I had seen spikes sticking up off the top. That was all I needed to see considering the amount of deer I had been seeing. I instantly looked for the shoulder and touched the musket off just as the deer was about to step out onto the dry land near where the fresh scrape was. Fire rolled out the end of the barrel, and then musket smoke rolled out into the opening where the deer was. The smoke hung there over the water in the dim light like a fog. With the mountains darkening in the distance it is one of those images that hunting sooner or later provides us with, to remain in our memories forever.

At the shot, the deer had bolted back across the water where it had come from. It cleared the entire expanse of the water only landing once in the middle of the pool with a large splash, and it was on land again the second time it came down. I got down from my stand, and what I found was a rather large clump of white fur floating on top of the water. My heart sank, I knew from experience that white hair doesn't come from anywhere good. I made my way around to the dry land where the deer had disappeared. It was getting down right dark now. I couldn't see any blood, and did not have a flash light or any other gear. I decided that I should make my way out to my truck, and if the deer was hit like I think he was, it would probably be a wise decision to let him sit anyway. Driving home I kept replaying the events in my head, and I just couldn't figure it out. The shot had felt good. The deer was quartering away, and was close enough that I just couldn't fathom hitting it poorly.

The next morning's first rays of light found me scouring the edge of the woods where last I had seen the deer the night before. Several more smaller clumps of white hair, one small drop of blood and then nothing. I circled, and scoured, but I found nothing else. Finding this deer would be a miracle, are the exact words that went through my head. I didn't think I stood a chance. Finally I just started to walk along in the direction where I had heard the deer fleeing. I tried to follow the path of least resistance. Better than 100 yards away I found a few drops of blood on some swale grass, and could see tracks crossing a small wet spot. From then on I started to find one drop of blood every five yards or so. With the loose dry leaves it was easy to miss a single drop of blood, and if one of the leaves had flipped over I wouldn't have any blood for 10 yards. It took plenty of circling to keep picking up on the sign especially if the deer had changed directions. I finally came to a big splotch in the leaves where he had laid down. I felt a little excitement again, but I was soon back to looking for specks of blood. I knew that the trail could dry up all together anytime. The buck had cut down along the edge of a brook obviously to get a drink of water, circled, and cut across its own backtrack to go at a 90-degree angle to the direction it had been traveling. With such little blood sign it took me 45 minutes to sort it all out. From there it headed straight up over a ridge, and as I've pointed out before, a wounded animal going uphill is generally not a good sign.

I was about a third of the way down the back of the ridge when I found the deer's bed again in some tight beech whips. There were only half a dozen drops of blood in it. I felt the bed and it did not feel warm to the touch, but as I proceeded forward the buck exploded out of the whips at the bottom of the hill, and disappeared into some thick hemlocks starting up another ridge. It happened too quickly to get a shot off, and I was shocked to find the animal still alive. What I noticed as I shouldered my gun was that it seemed to wiggle slightly. After intentionally applying pressure I realized that there was a significant wiggle where the butt stock attached to the muzzleloader's break open action. The gun obviously had a screw loose.

Now I'm not one to make excuses, and when I miss, I just admit it, but this went a long way toward explaining my poor shot placement. I hurried over to where I had seen the deer disappear, and could not find any sign of blood. I made my way to the top of the ridge crisscrossing all of the way trying to pick up on some blood sign. After spending 45 minutes scouring the area, and even going down the backside of the ridge to a large bog that the deer would not likely have crossed I was losing hope. I was walking the top of the ridge where I had seen the buck disappear, and was thinking he couldn't have much more than a scratch to still be running ridges after all this time. The highs and lows of the day, and the uncertainty of the outcome had my stomach in a knot, and I decided it was time to let go and admit defeat.

About that time I heard what sounded like a man's whistle. It went wee-woo, if you could make that sound into a whistle. I wasn't sure what I had heard so I gave a whistle back. Sure enough I got the whistle a second time, and then I heard what I thought were muffled voices. I had been tracking for five hours as it was around noon, and I did not know exactly where I was any more, but I was fairly certain that I would not be encountering any other people in this area. In fact, I was so certain, that I had not bothered to put on my hunter's orange, as it is optional in New Hampshire. The first thing I did was retrieve my orange from my pack and put it on, at which point I whistled again. I did not get a reply this time, but I was so certain of what I had heard that I yelled out "hello."

I proceeded to walk up a small knob toward some hemlocks to where I had heard the whistle. About half way there I looked down, and found the blood trail again. I walked on past it, to where I had a view down the entire side of the ridge through the open hardwoods, and apparently my "hello" had been greeted by nothing but wind, leaves, and trees as that was all I could see. Now whoever is reading this may be thinking that my gun wasn't the only one with a loose screw, but so help me, this is the way that the events transpired, as I interpreted them. It sounds far fetched, but I like to think that maybe Chick, uncle Louis, and Denis Wedge had opened a door from the other side, and let out a few whistles to draw my attention to the blood trail again, and a few muffled voices escaped before the door shut. Make what you want of it, but that's all I'm going to say about that.

I got on the trail again, and eventually lost it after a ways. I began to crisscross once again, working my way further down the ridge on the line the buck had been traveling. I was looking at the ground for blood as I traveled when sudden, close by, movement startled me to attention. It was the buck's attempt to get out of his bed at around eight yards. I was practically on top of him. His sudden movement had been matched by my own as I shouldered my rifle, and we both froze as he was unable to gain his feet. It seemed odd to be so close to a live wild deer. He was

no longer fleet of foot. I looked at him for a moment over the top of my scope, and whispered an apology for his predicament and then ended it.

I never did get a deer in Maine that year, so the venison from that spike horn was greatly appreciated. I got what I had asked for, the buck that had made the scrape near my stand. You oughta have seen the clodhoppers on that spike horn. He just plain had big feet. What I can't believe is that the coyote's hadn't got on his trail, and finished him off, as this area seemed to be filthy with them. Matter of fact, I took a few coyotes out of that area hoping to find one with a hair cut. I got a few nice ones, but not one that was missing any fur.

The "Loose screws buck" very near where he fell.

This coyote found himself in a little mid-winter predicament, compliments of the author. The fur of a mid-winter coyote is prime. It's thick and long, and you can about bury your hand in it. The pelts make a beautiful wall hanging for any trophy room. In my estimation, coyote trapping is one of the most challenging types of trapping. It also happens to be my favorite type of trapping.

Trapping a coyote in the winter with a foothold is even harder due to the ever-changing conditions of the snow. If the top of the snow melts a little due to sunshine, and then the surface freezes hard at night, the coyotes will run right over the top of the trap. Then you have to re-set the trap, and now the yotes are nervous because they can see sign in the snow that you've been there, and also they can smell that you have been there. It's a constant game that is ever changing with the weather, and the animals. When you finally "win" it's a thrill almost as intense as a successful deer hunt.

When I wrote this book, I wanted it to be mostly about hunting stories. I said "if I have to read one more article on how to hunt a scrape, I will have had all I can take." I want to follow along and look over the hunter's shoulder through his writing, and feel the excitement of the hunt as it unfolds. This is how I tried to write this book, but I believe it is important to briefly relate how the scrape relates to the hunter, and now seems to be a fitting time to do so.

This coyote weighed roughly 35 pounds. Notice how I'm holding it with one hand. Compare in size to the larger coyote and consider that I'm six foot one inch tall. I don't know how much he weighed, but we grow them big up here in New Hampshire. I've been told that they have wolf DNA, and I believe it. The "little" coyotes in the west don't take down deer, but you better believe they do here in the Northeast.

I'd like to talk a little about what a scrape is. A scrape is an area on the ground that a buck deer paws out. He'll clear out all of the leaves, and whatever debris happens to be around to expose bare dirt. From my experience this "bare spot" on the ground is generally 30 inches to three feet in diameter. The buck will usually urinate in this bare patch of ground, and oftentimes you can smell this if you put your nose to the dirt. I've collected this dirt to be used as a scent in other locations. Usually the scrape is created under a branch that is the right height for the deer to be able to rub the bases of his antlers, and eyes on. This releases gland scents that are unique to that buck, and some believe it is a way of communicating with other deer.

The breeding urge seems to trigger the desire in the buck deer to create a scrape. Most generally they are created during the fall "rut" or breeding season. Some of the experts say that these scrapes are like leaving a calling card for does, and when a doe in estrous urinates in the scrape this helps the buck to find her. I don't necessarily buy into that theory.

Hal Blood wrote a great book called *Hunting Big Woods Bucks*. As you might guess Hal is strictly a big buck hunter, and his book is a wealth of information on hunting large antlered, big bodied bucks in big woods. Hal's occupation is that of a guide. Hal doesn't just hunt around his work schedule, *it is his work schedule*. As a result I would say that he gets to spend more time in the woods observing the whitetail than the average hunter.

Oftentimes the articles about scrapes repeat the same information over and over just in a slightly different format. I believe Hal sheds a new light on the scrape as it relates to wild free ranging deer. Many times the "experts'" observations are in relation to fenced-in animals. In Hal's book he wrote a piece about scrapes that immediately made sense to me. He says that "bucks make scrapes because they are genetically imprinted to do so." He also says "In twenty years, only once have I seen a doe track around a scrape in the big woods. By the time a doe is ready to breed a buck will be standing there waiting." I believe this is true.

When a doe comes into estrous, the bucks are not going to be messing around with a scrape trying to find her. If the wind is right, he can probably smell her a mile away, and as Hal said, that buck will be waiting. The deer's nose is a far greater tool than most people give credit for. I believe a buck's nose is the tool used to find a doe that's ready to breed, not a scrape. A buck can travel downwind of an area with does in it and without setting foot in the area, he knows if a doe is starting to come into estrous.

Now that we know what a scrape is, and a little about why the buck makes it, I'd like to discuss briefly how it can be exploited by the hunter. You can generally see the buck's footprint in the exposed earth, and this gives you an idea of how large he is. It's been my experience that oftentimes scrapes are located on "edges" — the edge of a swamp, the edge of the hardwoods where they meet the darker growth or softwoods, the edge of a clearing or field. The scrape is a useful piece of information because you get an idea of what type of buck is in the area that you are hunting, and you also get an idea of where he has been or is traveling. If you keep tabs on the scrape you can start to figure out if he is freshening it up, and if so how often. Put together with other deer sign in the area (tracks, droppings) you can start to put the pieces of the puzzle together.

I know that it's getting off the subject of hunting a little bit, but any well-rounded hunter/gatherer should know how to catch lake trout for the table through the ice. Besides I'm not the only die-hard hunter that also enjoys hard-water fishing in the winter months. Hopefully you will gain something in the way of information to add to your lake trout fishing arsenal through the following story.

23

THE WINTER RITUAL

I sat peering out the window at the windblown frozen landscape. The dull gray sky, and frying venison had me reliving pleasant memories from the now distant hunting season. I had been sitting in the same spot for hours slowly twitching my right hand as I felt the small weight of my jig bouncing off the bottom when unexpectedly the hand-hewn wild cherry jig stick went wild in my hand, and was nearly torn from my grasp. Hours of quiet midwinter tranquility had been interrupted with an explosion of flailing hands as I pulled on the line, hand over fist. The head shaking struggle reverberated back up through the eight-pound test line. I felt he was going to break away, so I let the line slip through my fingers, watching that it did not catch on anything that would snag it up, and that it stayed clear of the cook stove. I was regaining line again, and he was getting close to the surface now. I caught a glimpse of him as he swam beneath the hole in the ice. He looked big, but then again they always do. The water seems to magnify their size. I was reaching the most critical juncture of the battle, getting the head started up through the hole when a burst of energy ripped line from my hand. As the line sizzled around the ice on the lower edge of the hole, I felt a pop, and the line went limp. I peered in disbelief down through the hole, and into the deep dark beyond as the agony of defeat set in.

Lake trout fishing for me is the midwinter ritual, hours of monotony broken up by seconds of pure adrenaline insanity. Sometimes I fish all day for that one bite, and other times I'm blessed with several bites, but they are never so plentiful that messing one up is forgivable. Some people prefer to fish the smaller warm water ponds where you're allowed up to six lines. The perch and pickerel fishing is usually fast and furious in these places, but winter for me is a slower paced time for reflection, and relaxation. I'd rather not run around like a chicken with my head cut off trying to tend six lines, but prefer to set off on my own out on the big lakes where you're allowed only two lines. The fishing is much slower, but like trapping coyotes in the snow, or anything that's a little more challenging, success is that much sweeter when it finally comes.

One of my favorite trout lakes is New Hampshire's Lake Winnipesaukee, which is located about 15 minutes from my house. Big trout lurk in these waters. My personal best catches are in the four- to five-pound range, but every year people catch them 10 and 12 pounds, and bigger. Lake Winnipesaukee is a big draw for fisherman and tourists alike, and is well known and written about as a fishing spot. Another "secret" less-known spot is Great East Lake. It's a border lake between Maine and New Hampshire, and is fishable on either state's license. It's only located about 20 minutes from the southern end of Lake

Winnipesaukee. The locals will probably hang me for telling, but I believe it to be the best kept secret, and the best lake trout fishery in New Hampshire. Many people don't care to fish for lake trout because they seem difficult to catch. Over the years, I've developed a foolproof way for targeting and catching lake trout. If you follow a few simple techniques combined with a little persistence, you too can have success fishing for lake trout.

A closeup of my hand made bottom-baiter, and jig stick for those of you who might take a notion to build these things. The bottom baiter is very basic. It consists of brass sheet metal (to avoid rust) and a brass hinge. Holes are drilled in the "compartment" but not in the "trap door." The baiter fills with water, and when the string attached to the baiter is yanked, the weight of the water against the solid "trap door" pushes it open releasing the bait. Notice there is and extra sheet of brass laminated on the door to add weight. The clip on the door is easily bent to adjust how tightly it "hugs" on the piece of metal dowel used as a catch on the other side. I personally soldered the components together, but other methods could be used such as rivets or small bolts.

TACKLE/GEAR

I try to keep my gear simple. I prefer to jig for trout, I always use a tip up with a live smelt (the lake trout's primary food source) for my second line, but I rarely put that jig stick down even for a second. The people that have trouble catching trout usually fish with tip ups, but you will out fish them five bites to their one with your jig stick. A jig stick need not be anything fancy, a stick with a notch in each end to wrap line around will do the trick. Make sure your notches are exactly one foot apart, and you will be able to keep track of how much water you are fishing over as you let out line.

I've had my best luck in 40 to 60 feet of water, but have regularly caught them much deeper, and I know people that consistently target waters 20 feet or shallower. I use heavy nylon line with a swivel at the end, followed by 12 feet of eight-pound mono attached directly to a jig. I've developed so much confidence in my jig that I only carry two, both of them the same size and make. One to fish with, and one for a backup. The jig I use is a Swedish pimple about the size of your pinky finger with a glow in the dark strip on it. I hook the tail end half of a smelt on to the jig's hook.

In New Hampshire, if a jig is used in combination with bait, the treble hook must be replaced by a single hook. I also use a homemade bottom baiter, which is perhaps the biggest secret weapon of all. I place these few simple things into a brown ash pack basket along with some venison , and something to cook it with for lunch, and I'm confident that I can catch lake trout.

The day of the missed fish previously described started out in the darkness of the early morning as my fishing excursions usually do. After a one half-mile hike, I reached my fishing destination, a spot that over the years has proven itself to be a consistent trout producing area. The first thing I do is chop a hole with my ice chisel, and place my tip up, this way I'm fishing while I chop my jig hole, and set up my portable shelter.

Yes I prefer to chop my holes; there's something to be said for simplicity. You'll be amazed at how quickly a razor sharp chisel will burrow its way through

226

the ice. You won't be choking on exhaust fumes, or ruining the quiet of the serene winter landscape with an exhaust belching power auger. If the ice is thick, and you get to gasping for that lung-burning, frigid winter air, so much the better — the extra exercise is a refreshing way to start a fishing trip — it gets the blood flowing and the senses alert. An ice chisel is much lighter to carry than a power auger, and you don't have to worry about it breaking down, or carrying gas.

The portable ice shelter is not necessary, and I fished for years without it, but it sure makes life comfortable, not to mention that you will fish longer because you are warm, so one might argue that it makes you more productive as well. It also doubles as a sled to drag your gear on. Once the shelter is set up your cook stove will keep you warm as well as cook your food. Now you're ready to start jigging, and enjoying the solitude.

My cousin Nick, one of my best, good fishing buddies, roasting venison and fresh caught lake trout over an open fire on a beautiful mid-March day out on the ice.

Before jigging, I like to bait the bottom of the lake with a homemade bottom-baiter. I chop up a few smelts, and lower them to the bottom. Once on the bottom, I pull the baiter up about seven feet, and yank the string, which releases the trap door and the bait. By bringing it up a few feet off the bottom the bait spreads out over a bigger area instead of being released in a small pile. It's important not to put too much junk down the hole. Three or four chopped up smelts or shiners is plenty. Every few hours, or if I get a bite, I repeat the process. I believe when the trout comes along, he gets into a bit of a feeding frenzy with the chopped up bait, and then when he happens upon your jig, he sucks it in without hesitation.

Two good sized lake trout.

This is also a great way to catch freshwater cusk, who are also bottom dwellers. The cusk kind of looks like a cross between an eel and a catfish. Cusk can grow to large proportions, and are noted for their use in chowder as the meat has a tendency to hold together and not fall apart. The trout, and cusk oftentimes run together, I've been pulling a trout up, and had a guy sitting beside me pulling a cusk up at the same time. When you go hours between bites, and catch two fish together like that, it's not a coincidence. If I catch a cusk, I'm trying to get that fish off, and get my jig back down to the bottom as quickly as possible.

TECHNIQUE

The last thing I want to talk about is technique. I've taken new people out fishing, and inevitably as they sit there on an overturned five-gallon bucket, the first thing they seem to want to do is jig that stick repeatedly from ice level to eye level. I believe that such movement would scare the dickens out of any respectable trout. I prefer a much more subtle movement, almost a twitch if you will. The end of your jig stick shouldn't be moving much more than an inch or two. Bring the jig up, and watch it as you impart action on it. You want it to look like an injured broken baitfish that's twitching out the last of its life; the tail end of the smelt you hooked on will flutter around a little bit. Fish within six inches of the bottom — this technique is deadly on lake trout.

If I feel anything abnormal, I set the hook. Most times it's not a subtle thing. They usually hit it like a freight train, but sometimes the weight of your jig will be gone and will feel as though nothing is there, like your jig broke off or something. Set the hook. The fish has grabbed the jig, and ran up slightly off the bottom with it. Many times you'll feel a slight flutter of the jig, and this is the only time that I can predict a bite. The only thing I can figure is the trout comes in first, swats the bait with his tail to stun it, and then comes back to suck it in. Inevitably after that little flutter (and I've even said it out loud, "here it comes"), within five seconds I'll have a fish battling at the other end of the line, but mostly they just hit it like a freight train.

Remember be patient and persistent, don't get lazy, and stop jigging for a while with the idea that "at least I have a tip up in." I can't overstress enough how important that jig stick is for targeting lake trout. I don't put that stick down for one minute. I cook and eat with one hand, but the other is constantly jigging. If you stop for even a few minutes, that trout could swim by, and the hours of effort will have been for nothing.

REDEMPTION

After the disastrous loss of my hard-earned lake trout, described in the first paragraph, I grabbed my ice chisel and knocked off the sharp edge at the bottom of the hole that my line had snapped on. I muttered under my breath as I scolded myself for making such a rookie mistake, all the while irritatingly tearing off and chewing chunks of venison with one hand while I jigged with the other. I pouted for the next couple of hours, when finally it happened again.

It doesn't matter how many trout you've caught, you'll never get used to jigging for hours, and suddenly having what feels to be a lead weight tugging at the other end. It always catches you off guard, and it always charges you with a sudden rush of adrenaline-fueled excitement. I took extra care handling this fish, if he made off with my last jig, I'd have to go home. I didn't deserve it after my sinful ignorance in losing the first fish, but felt as though I had redeemed myself just the same as my 23 inches of lake trout dinner writhed around at my feet. Give lake trout fishing a try this winter, you'll either get bored quickly and hate it, or you'll be like me, and savor every outing.

**Two keeper lake trout caught while wearing my
lucky wool hat made by Cindy Green.**

24

EAT WILD BE WILD

When I started trapping, I learned that there was more to look for in the woods than just deer tracks. The more you learn about the woods and all of its inhabitants, and how they interact with each other, as well as the land they live on, the better outdoorsman and, ultimately, deer hunter you will become. As a result your time spent afield will be much more rewarding. It seems that the aspect of hunting to put good quality meat in the freezer is rarely emphasized, and takes a back seat to the trophy aspect of big antlers. Don't get me wrong, I love big antlers, and it adds to the experience greatly if I get a nice buck, but the meat, and the satisfaction of providing for yourself directly from the land is way overlooked. The meat aspect of the hunt should be emphasized as equally and as often as is antler size. Venison is high in protein, and is low in fat, which means it is very good for you.

I'm an independent person, and like to do, and provide for myself as much as possible. Though getting away from "the man" and the "system" entirely, and still remaining a functioning member of society is almost impossible, I still try to do so as much as possible. Providing my own meat is just one more way of doing that. Many people reject venison because it doesn't come neatly packaged in Styrofoam from the grocery store. The fact is that you don't know where store bought meat has been, what chemicals it was treated with or what kind of chemicals or hormones that the animal was treated with. I know where my meat has been, and how it was taken care of. People have more of a tendency to do a good job if they know the meat they are processing is going into there own mouths.

I'm no expert on the subject, but I've heard it argued that vegetables that are mass produced are grown in the same soil over and over again, and that certain nutrients in the soil are depleted. Now the vegetables need fertilizers and other chemicals to grow. Over time this lack of mother nature produced nutrients can become a deficiency in the human body, and results in poor health, and a compromised immune system that eventually leads to disease. These mass-produced vegetables are engineered, as are many of the animals from cows to chickens, to produce the best profits as with any business. The tomatoes are treated with chemicals to make them red, or pleasing to the eye, the chickens made to produce many eggs, and so on. Unfortunately they are being engineered for profits and not necessarily to be healthy.

If you get your food directly from nature, perhaps, your getting some of these nutrients that you are lacking as a result of eating mass-produced food? Again I'm no expert, but from a common sense stand point it sounds reasonable to me. More healthy lean food could eventually lead to weight loss which could lead to more energy and a clearer mental focus. Wow! Let's go hunting, and gathering.

FIDDLEHEADS

In the springtime fiddlehead ferns can be gathered by the bushel basket full if you find a lucrative patch, and the good news is that they come up in the same place year after year. Many people keep their fiddlehead patch a closely guarded secret. I generally freeze enough to last the better part of a year with use at the occasional meal. Fiddleheads are delicious, and keep very well if they are shrink-wrapped with a food saver. If your going to be a hunter and gatherer you need a food saver. It keeps all frozen food fresher longer. I've had many meals of fiddleheads, venison and wild mushrooms. Fiddleheads come up in the springtime around mothers day in my region.

Fiddleheads are smooth and have an emerald green color. Most other inedible ferns are not smooth, but are covered in a hair-like substance.

Elbridge Russell (mentioned in the chapter entitled Hunt Alone Or With Friends) says that when the poplar tree's buds break open, they release a pollen that floats on the breeze and you know that the soil temperature, and all of the other conditions are perfect, and the fiddleheads are ready to be picked. Don't pass this tidbit of information over, or read it quickly and dismiss it. This is the type of local knowledge that the seasoned woodsman brings to the table. The average person wouldn't have a clue what a little piece of pollen floating on the breeze meant. I did not personally know this, and I am learning a great deal through others by writing this book. Any time I can learn a little bit of information about the natural world that I did not know, I consider it another little gem that I store away in my treasure book of knowledge. It helps put another tiny little piece of the puzzle that makes up the natural world in place. This is the type of local "secret" that I am trying to expose for all to see, and what I mean when I say that you will learn things from this book that you will not learn in most other hunting books. This information serves a good purpose. Fiddleheads are best picked after they have broken through the soil, and when they are still coiled tightly, and close to the ground. After they have unraveled into a fern they are not a desired edible. As a result sometimes there is a very short time window in which to pick the fiddleheads. Many times the best fiddlehead patches require a fair bit of effort to get to, either by hiking or boating. You can start to see how this information becomes useful. It enables you to really zero in on when the time is right instead of having to make multiple trips to check, and worse yet, possibly miss them if they go by. Bill Frasier gauges when the fiddleheads are ready for picking by a different method. He feeds the birds, and when he sees his very first hummingbird of the year, he knows he can go get a basket full of fiddleheads.

Look for fiddleheads in sandy soil near the banks of, or in the flood plain of a river. One of the fiddleheads growing requirements is that it needs to flood yearly. You can no doubt find more info on line. Be sure that you have positively identified any, and all plants, and mushrooms before you eat them as there are some that will not only make you very sick, but also a few that will positively kill you.

BERRIES

Every year I take a family vacation up near the Canadian border in northern New Hampshire toward the end of July. Much of the land is owned by paper companies, and the result is a lot of clear cuts that are ideal for raspberries and moose. Each day I'm out at daylight to pick berries while my wife, and daughter sleep in. I get to have quiet alone time spent in nature while gathering something delicious to eat, and am quite often rewarded with a moose sighting. I'm generally back around 8:30 or 9:00 just in time for a big home made breakfast and lazy morning around camp with Alyssa, and Isabelle. How can life get any better than that? I try to gather several gallons and freeze them to last as long as possible. My favorite thing to do with the berries is to add them to vanilla ice cream with a little milk, and make a shake out of them in the blender. Later in the summer I collect blackberries near home, and also we generally have a year's supply of blueberries for our pancakes, which Alyssa, and little Isabelle enjoy helping me collect as we have a lucrative spot on a mountainside with beautiful views as a bonus.

FISHING

Another midsummer activity that provides lots of stress relieving fun, and healthy wild food is fishing. Lately I've been fishing with Bill Frasier out on the ocean several times throughout the course of the summer. Bill's a great hunter with many whitetails to his credit, and some nice bucks as well. Unlike me Bill takes his fishing just as seriously as his hunting. Depending on the tide we sometimes leave as early as 2:00 A.M. The rising sun finds us tearing across the surface of the salty water following Bills GPS to the cod, and haddock fishing grounds on Jeffreys Ledge 25 miles offshore. Bill's got this fishing hammered down to a science, and he rarely disappoints. Most days it seems more like catching than it does fishing, and I can honestly say that I've never come home without something to eat.

**The 26 pound cod taken while fishing with Bill
Frasier on Jeffreys Ledge 25 miles offshore.**

The whale watching can be unbelievable. On one day the herring were bubbling all over the surface of the water in patches that were several acres in size. Pretty soon a huge ring of roiling bubbles would appear in the middle of the herring that would be an aqua marine color in contrast to the dark herring filled water around it. This bubbling was a humpback whale that would emerge up through the middle of the baitfish with its mouth wide open. The momentum would carry the enormous animal half of its 50-foot length straight up out of the water into the air, boat-swallowing mouth agape, before it fell over sideways in a titanic splash. It's both awe inspiring as well as intimidating to have this type of activity happening within yards of the boat.

Occasionally a wake would appear headed for a school of herring, and a whales back would emerge out of the water like a submarine bearing down on the bait-fish. Herring would rooster tail 10 or 15 feet or more into the air off from the whales back as he slammed into the herring. We had whales swim just a couple of feet under the water so close to the boat that you could see their eye, and blowhole. It's truly amazing to see the food chain in action on such a grand scale.

Many days we're back at the dock at sunset with a cooler of fillets so heavy that we literally need a dolly to wheel the cooler up the dock to the truck. It makes for a long day, but it's well worth it. Fresh fish is healthy, and delicious food, and it provides many meals in the quantities I catch it in with Bill. My personal best cod caught with Bill was 26 pounds, and he put up an epic battle. If Bill ever invites you to go fishing, make the time to take him up on it.

SALTWATER SMELT

A good wintertime activity that puts some delicious fish on the plate is saltwater smelting on the tidal rivers of Maine and New Hampshire. Smelting is generally done through the ice. The targeted fish is the saltwater smelt. It is the same smelt that inhabits the fresh water lakes, only the sea-run variety grow a fair bit larger. The freshwater smelt generally doesn't get much bigger than 3-5 inches though there are exceptions. Saltwater smelt generally average twice that size. Fishing is usually better after dark, and it's not uncommon to catch 100 fish in a night.

Most people prefer to rent an ice shanty for a nominal fee from a business that puts out dozens of them for the purpose of renting. These ice shacks are usually lined up so there is only a few feet in between. It's not uncommon to see 20 or 30 of them all in a little cluster. Generally a wood stove is provided for heat, and doubles as a source for cooking. Smelt have small mouths, and sometimes bite very lightly. Small hooks baited with bits of sea worms are used, and when a slight tapping of the line is detected, the fish are hand lined to the surface. Most times the fishing is best when the tide is moving. This is a great way to spend a midwinter night. It's a chance to relive past hunts with family, and friends while the venison sears on the wood stove, and the smelt pile up in the bucket for more wild meals to come.

Be prepared for the possibility that the food might not be the only thing that is wild in these "smelting villages." Those good ol' New England boys can get to hootin, and hollerin, sometimes even fighting. It's most generally interesting if not entertaining. Bill Frasier tells of a brawl that got so intense he turned out his light, but then it occurred to him that they could probably see the smoke coming from his stovepipe. One thing is for darn sure, if your bringing a lady she'd best not have sensitive ears.

MUSHROOMS

Nature has all kinds of little secrets, and hides treasures that are sometimes very tasty. Wild edible mushrooms are one of nature's very rewarding little treasures to find. I would recommend caution here as there are several varieties that are poisonous, and a few that are lethal. There are some very good field guides on the subject, and you might even seek out someone who can show you what to look for. There are groups, and clubs that go on mushroom walks. I've been on a few of these walks, and listened to a man talk that was very knowledgeable about mushrooms.

Mushrooms are made up mostly of protein which is similar to meat. Mushrooms should be handled like meat, refrigerated, etc. Some of these proteins are proteins that we don't get any where else in our diet, and he talked a lot about mushrooms having qualities that might prevent cancer. Once we reach adulthood, we've generally eaten all of the different types of food, and found out what we're allergic to. After positively identifying an edible mushroom, you should try a little, and wait 24 hours to confirm that you are not allergic, or going to have some other type of reaction. It's unlikely, but this is something entirely knew that has never entered your body before. There are several varieties of wild mushrooms that are very easy to identify, and that can't be easily confused with anything else. At least three easily identified edibles that I know of occur during hunting season.

The first one that I learned to identify on my own, thanks to David Haine, is the oyster mushroom. This type of mushroom takes a little looking, but is fairly common. Oyster mushrooms grow in a shelf-like pattern on the side of dead wood or standing trees, and often come back in the same place year after year. They almost resemble an oyster shell hence the name. They are colored anywhere from white to a light tan, and occasionally brownish color. They are the mainstays of my wild mushroom diet as I generally am able to gather them in fairly large quantities. From what I gather, they like cool weather followed by warm, wet or humid conditions. These conditions occur frequently in the fall, and this is when I find the majority of my oysters. In my region I start looking for them in October, and continue finding them when conditions are favorable, right up until freeze up.

Again the more you learn about the natural world the more rewarding your time spent hunting will be. I still remember the excitement of an afternoon muzzleloader hunt on an autumn day in New Hampshire. No, I didn't get or even see a deer on this hunt but I found oyster mushrooms for the first time on my own. I had a deer in the freezer from a tag that I had filled in Maine. So in the following days I enjoyed several meals of wild mushrooms, and venison, which brought a great deal of satisfaction from the time spent afield on the "unsuccessful" deer hunt.

I wear a backpack when I hunt, and always have a plastic bag stashed, and extra room in the pack's main compartment for something I may want to bring home, like mushrooms. The oyster mushrooms can be found growing in large quantities at times. I've filled as much as two plastic shopping bags full from a single tree.

The next type of mushroom that I would mention is the sulphur shelf, or chicken mushroom. Its bright colors make it easy to spot. It is bright yellow, and bright orange, and can be found growing on the side of dead oak trees. My own personal experience is that you want to find this mushroom when it is young. The older the mushroom gets the more woody, and less tender it becomes. When found at the right stage of the game this is also a very good eating mushroom. Though my field guides list this as a fall mushroom, I've found it in my region from spring right on through to the fall.

There are many edible varieties of wild mushrooms that can be found from spring right through the summer months, but the last one I will mention can also be found during hunting season. It's called the "hen of the woods," and is a fair bit harder to find than the other mushrooms I mentioned. This is truly an elusive treasure, and also the best tasting mushroom of the three listed. Bill Russell's field guide to mushrooms claims that "recent scientific research confirms ancient Asian belief that the hen of the woods mushroom offers a wide range of health giving benefits." Its scarcity and unique nutty, almost earthy flavor, make it a highly sought after, and most desirable prize. I can assure you that you'll be really happy with yourself if you find this delicious edible mushroom sitting on your plate next to your venison.

The Hen can be a rather large shelf-like mushroom, and is usually found on very old, and very large, oak or maple trees, oftentimes near the base of the tree. Unlike the other mushrooms mentioned this one is more camouflaged, and blends into its surroundings well making it easy to miss. It's generally a brownish tan color on top, and the underside is cream in color. Again once you find the tree that it grows on, you can generally return year after year and reap the rewards.

This pretty well raps up a year's worth of wild food hunting, and gathering. I know the deer I eat lead a wild and humane life, had a humane end, and ate wild things provided by nature. If you eat enough of it you may start to feel a little wild yourself, I know I do. I've got the wild in me, do you have it in you? Have you started to get the idea yet that the meat part of the hunt is very important to me? Good. Antlers are thrilling, but the meat is also a very satisfying aspect of the hunt. I think most of us, at one time or another, have been to the fancy shmancy restaurant, and seen the venison tenderloin on the menu for $40 a plate. This is probably farm-raised venison. Next time you have wild delicious deer meat in the freezer, don't take it for granted, make good use of it.

I read an article written by Dave Peterson on finding, and eating wild mushrooms. The following quote was taken from that article. **"Gathering and eating from nature are ancient sacred acts. To kill and waste is sinful, stupid, and ugly."**

While we're talking about the benefits of eating wild foods, I think it's worthwhile to mention that I don't recommend using drugs or alcohol in any capacity. They will make you weak minded, and eventually weak of the body as well. I feel that they will rob you of any benefit that you may acquire through eating natural foods. People who don't use drugs or alcohol can expect the following qualities if they desire them: sharpness, focus, drive, physical fitness, clarity. These qualities may not pay off in a week's time, but over the long term they will have a huge benefit on your life. You will be more successful in everything that you do. Now I'll list some of the qualities that people can very easily develop if they get sucked in to using alcohol or drugs on a regular basis. Overweight, sloppy, lethargic, unreliable, laziness. Which qualities would you like to describe you?

If you are interested in learning how to identify, and find wild edible mushrooms, I would recommend that you get several field guides. The info provided here about mushrooms is mainly meant to spark your interest so that perhaps you will seek out someone who can show you. Many people don't realize that these little delicacies grow in our woods, and hopefully it will spur you to further investigation. One of my favorite guides, and a great place to start is called *Field Guide to Wild Mushrooms of Pennsylvania and the Mid-Atlantic*, by Bill Russell. This guide encompasses the entire northeast region as well. I've learned more about mushroom hunting from this one book than any of the others, but I recommend several mushroom guides. Happy hunting.

> *A man of many friends comes to ruin, but there is a friend who sticks closer than a brother.* ~ *Prov. 18:24*

25

JAKE'S RIVER

Jake was a rottweiler, and no, he wasn't a hunting dog. You might wonder what business he has in a hunting book. Well, he picked hunting season to die, so I think that qualifies him. He was with me 11 years, and he could sense the love of the hunt in me. He had learned to anticipate the shortening days, the crisp mornings, and the smell of fall in the air that would soon be associated with the joyous celebration, and electricity in the air that goes along with bringing home a deer.

Jake was bought by my dad for the amount of $50. The story goes that he was a pure bred that was the result of two neighbors breeding their dogs. He was just a tiny little thing that would curl up in the crook of my arm when dad first brought him home. The large paws on the little puppy hinted at how large he might grow. Dad gave him his "handle," and over the course of the following weeks the dog seemed to take a liking to me. I was getting ready to move out of my dad's house, and considering Jake's favor toward me, dad let me have him. I didn't realize at the time what a friend that dog would become, and how strong the bond between a dog and a man could be. They truly are man's best friend. They are completely loyal. They don't hold a grudge if you do them wrong, they forgive you immediately. We used to keep Jake in a crate at night when he was a growing puppy to help potty train him. Now, most dogs hate the crate, but Jake would readily run into it. I remember one time I climbed into his crate to see how he would react. I just barely fit in with my head and shoulders poking out. He got mad, and pouted, and I knew then he was a different kind of dog.

So Jake and I moved out together into our first apartment. It wasn't anything special, as a matter of fact most people might consider it to be somewhat of a rough lifestyle. We had no furniture when we first moved out, and it was the beginning of January. The apartment was lacking in many respects including insulation. The floor consisted of a rug laid over a concrete slab, and being that I didn't have any furniture, I slept on the floor in a sleeping bag with Jake curled up beside me. It was so cold that his water bowl would have a thin layer of ice in the morning, and the plumbing constantly froze. Tap water came from a brook out back, which meant that drinking water had to be bought. You might say all of this toughened us up a little bit, but Jake made a long cold winter tolerable.

I was in the beginning stages of becoming a chainsaw woodcarver during this time. I was self employed, which meant that Jake got to go to work with me every day. Basically, everywhere I went, Jake went. The second winter in the apartment, I bought a used snow machine to go ice fishing with, but my usual fishing buddy, Jake, would have no part of getting on that snow machine. I decided one day that Jake was going to get on that snow machine, but he was still pretty well dead set against the idea. Somewhat of a commotion ensued, and if I was honest, I'd have to say I got the worst of it.

We eventually developed a mutual respect for one another. I never tried to get him on that snow machine again, but he would run behind it following me for miles. It was because of exercise like this that Jake eventually became a thickly muscled 130-pound dog. I used to lie down on the floor, and he would flop all 130 pounds down smack on top of me, and just lay there while I patted him, until I decided that I needed to breathe again.

I remember once I had him tied out back next to the little river that runs behind the woodshop that I now own. At the time, the guy that owned the shop previously to me was out back teasing Jake. He was calling him to come even though he was tied up. Jake came running, but instead of hitting the end of his chain and snapping back like the guy thought he would, he hit the end of his chain, and snapped the linkage connecting it to his collar. The next thing I knew, the guy comes around the corner saying, "my God that's a rugged dog." Jake seemed to be somewhat of a knucklehead and I didn't realize it at the time, but looking back, so was I. He was going to have to be hard headed to ride shotgun with me for 11 years while I was going through my twenties. We grew up together, Jake and I.

Jake was still a young dog when I first purchased my woodcarving shop, and at just 24, I still had a lot of puppy in me. Jake would tear through that shop and knock over woodcarvings, and whatever else was in his way. Being that Jake was black, one of his favorite tricks was to lie somewhere amongst the black bear woodcarvings, and when a customer would come close by he would move, and in so doing startle the unsuspecting customer. The response was always the same, "I thought he was a wood carving." That's how he came to acquire the nick name "Bear Dog." One of Jake's favorite things was little girls with ice cream cones. It took some doing, but I finally broke him of that one.

Some people were intimidated, or afraid of him. Occasionally some city girl would run screaming for her car, and Jake would just sit there with a baffled look on his face. He didn't know he was a big scary dog. Truth is, he was just a big baby in a gorilla suit. Most people had a positive response, and wanted to pat him. Almost everybody was amazed at the size of him, especially the city people coming through who had never had a dog, or if they did a very small one. He liked to lean on or up against people, and when he did they could feel the weight of his heavy muscle, and many people would be thrown off balance. I guess it was fitting, country boys are supposed to have big dogs. Just like country boys are supposed to have four-wheel drive pick-up trucks. There's lots of good memories of tearing down dirt country roads with my dog sitting next to me in the cab of my truck, and I've got to tell you I miss him. We were always together, if it wasn't at work, then, we would be out in the woods during the off season hiking and scouting for deer sign.

We came a long ways together, that dog and I. We left my dad's house together with no money. We had nothing but dreams and ambition. I bought a business, and during his lifetime tripled the physical size of the building. He saw me get married to my wonderful wife, Alyssa. Alyssa and I bought a lake house that had been in her family. I still remember when Jake and I moved from our apartment into the lake house with Alyssa. It was like going from cold, and harsh to soft, warm and gentle. I knew Jake felt as spoiled as I did, I could tell by the way he would sack out on his fancy knew bed each night, and with his eyes closed not move a muscle as he soaked in the warmth that would put him to sleep. We were becoming "domesticated."

Women are not always all that keen on things that shed, but I think he eventually won over the lady of the house. It wasn't too much time that passed, and we had a little girl we named Isabella, a.k.a. Lil Goose. Jake was blessed with seeing her for the first three years of her life. We were a little nervous about bringing her home to such a large animal as Jake, and were concerned about him having jealousy issues where he might not feel like the baby anymore. We had set Isabella down in her stroller not long after she came home from the hospital, and we left the room for a few minutes. When I came back in, Jake had set his tennis ball right next to her in the stroller. I knew right then that everything was going to be fine. Jake was very protective of his ball, and would rarely let anybody near it.

Even though Jake was a family dog, and was friendly, and would take a pat on the head from anybody, he was still a one person dog. There was no doubt that he was my dog. He really didn't listen to anybody except for me. When let outside to do his business, Jake didn't always come back when Alyssa would call for him. Matter of fact, she could yell at the top of her lungs, and whistle till she was blue in the face, and if that dog didn't want to come in, he wouldn't. All I had to do was stick my head out the door and give a little Psst, Psst, barely audible, and he'd come running. He was a loyal dog.

Jake didn't like water. He'd even put off going outside as long as he possibly could if it was raining out. He would make great efforts to run around mud puddles so as not to get his feet wet. As you might expect, I never tried to get him into the lake as I'm sure it would be the snow machine incident all over. One summer day we had some friends at the house, and we all went for a swim. Jake was left on the beach, and we decided to swim out a considerable distance to a rock that we could stand on. Pretty soon somebody yelled, "Hey, look at Jake." He was swimming for all he was worth, with a look of sheer terror in his eyes. His loyalty to follow me where I went was strong indeed. I turned around, and swam back to shore with him.

As Jake started to get older, he mellowed out, and spent more time sleeping than tearing around knocking stuff over. In the last few years of his life he stopped coming to work every single day. I whistled at him every day. Some days he would bounce up, and come, and other days he'd just lay there. I figured that meant he needed a day off, so I'd let him stay home. The last year of his life he became a little stiff and sore, but he still managed to come to work every other day. He'd become somewhat of a celebrity up at the woodshop. People would stop every year to see him on there way to vacation in the White Mountains of New Hampshire. On the days that he wasn't there somebody would inevitably stop and ask about him. I think some people got a bigger kick out of seeing him than the woodcarvings.

Jake stopped eating for a few days, so I took him to the vet. Even though I knew he was very old for his breed, it still came as a shock when the vet told me Jake probably only had a week to live. Over the course of that night he had deteriorated to the point that he was having trouble walking. The next day I picked him up and put him in the truck for what I knew would probably be his last trip to the shop. He had been a woodshop dog his whole life, and I wanted him to smell the inside of the woodshop one more time, the freshly cut pine mixed with the aroma of wood preservatives, and to hear the chainsaws roar again. He had become as much a part of this special place as I had.

As soon as I heard the news from the vet, I knew where he should be buried — across the river — across the little river from where he used to be tied as a puppy, behind the shop, up next to the big boulder. It really isn't much of a river, more like a small brook. The brook hides folded between its currents, and tucked neatly and properly up under the bank, small shadows of speckled native brilliance that can occasionally be seen, but only by the trained eye, darting out for morsels of nourishment. It's a small tributary to the Chocorua River that has its origin up near the top of Mt. Chocorua, which lies in the White Mountain National Forest. Jake would drink there, and quench his thirst with that clear, cold mountain water. He'd sit there on the bank and bark at whatever he could smell in the woods beyond.

As far as I know, the flowage didn't previously have a name, but I'm naming it now after Jake. Jake's River. I brought his bed to work that day and placed it in front of the heater on the wide pine floor boards I'd milled myself. He lay resting there in front of the heater while I dug a hole for him outback, across the river. It was one of the first cold days of the year, and the raw, damp wind spit snow from the overcast sky as I shoveled.

The next couple of days I spent as much time with Jake as I could. I fed him small amounts of raw venison scraps from a deer I had recently killed in New

York to help keep his energy up some as he wouldn't eat anything else. Throughout the course of his life his most favorite thing in the whole world was to be patted on the head by me, and told what a good dog he was, you could just see him soak it in and bask in it. So that's what I did. I curled up next to him on the floor for hours, and told him what a good dog he was.

I decided the day before deer season that it was time. Some people might think it was just a coincidence that Jake was dying at the start of deer season, but I don't. He may have made it another day or two, but he was struggling, and I knew I wouldn't be there to comfort him. At first I thought I might drop him off at the vets, and come back to get him after he'd passed, because being the big tough guy that I am, I didn't want anybody to see me cry. That dog had stood beside me through everything, and I knew that seeing him through to the end was the right thing to do. I wasn't about to let him down.

A lot of things had changed about Jake. He was a shell of the dog that he once was at less than 100 pounds, and he had grayed slightly around the muzzle. As his heavy snout lay on my lap at the vets, I noticed that his eyes had not changed. He still looked up at me with that same unconditional love, and loyalty that he always had, even as the needle slipped into his vein. I was patting him on the head, telling him what a good dog he was, and he was basking and soaking it in as I watched the last little flickers of life leave his body. I hope my master is as kind to me in death. Jake, you weren't nothing but a good ol boy. Farewell old man, I'll see you across the river.

Jake and me when we were both young.

About the Author and His Philosophy

I have a wife, Alyssa, and four-year-old little girl, Isabella, A.K.A. Lil Goose, I love them both dearly, everything that I do is for them. They truly are the best part of my life.

I enjoy the outdoors, and find it tough to stay out of the woods even when it's not hunting season. I'm late for work far too often because a half hour in the woods turns into three hours in the woods. People talk about freedom a lot, but we're not truly free. We're all slaves to the system in some capacity, some more than others. The more we keep ourselves in debt the worse it is (pay off those credit cards, and fancy vehicles). Whether we realize it or not, or want to admit it or not, this is true. Laws, rules and regulations are constantly being imposed on us whether we like them, or agree with them or not. Our freedoms are constantly eroding.

"None are more hopelessly enslaved than those who falsely believe they are free,"   *~ Goethe*

Alone in the woods you're as close to free as your going to get. You're your own person, and make your own decisions. If you make a bad decision, you will deal with the consequences. This teaches responsibility. There is nobody standing over your shoulder telling you what you can and cannot do. It's refreshing, relaxing, a retreat from the rat race, and a place to recharge the batteries.

I find everything intriguing in the wild places — plants, animals, fungus (mushrooms), moss, wood and even stone. As a woodworker, I'm constantly intrigued by the different formations of the trees. Nature is full of little treasures if you know where to look. I turn bowls on the lathe. Because the crotch of a tree is constantly flexing with the wind, it oftentimes creates a beautiful pattern in the grain of the wood that in turn makes a beautiful wooden bowl. It's a part of the tree that is not turned into lumber, and is even tough to split for firewood.

To most, the crotch of a tree is useless, but to me a thing of beauty and also value lurks beneath the bark. It's a great feeling to create something of value from an object that many consider useless. Nature has continually tested the tree's strength with the wind making it tough, and difficult to split, and in so doing created a scar, or inner character. People are not all that different. Inner strength, and toughness can be hard qualities but good qualities.

I derive a good deal of my food from the wilderness, I recreate in the woods, and as a chainsaw sculptor, I earn my living from the wilderness as well. I feel a strong connection to the wild places. Not only do I make bowls, and carvings with logs, but I also have a sawmill that I turn trees into lumber with, and lumber into rustic furniture. I can also say that I heated my house 100 percent with firewood this year, not a drop of oil was used to heat my home. If you've ever heated entirely with firewood, you know it hardens the body, it's good for you, it makes you sleep well at night. Besides sleeping well it makes you appreciate a belly full of that wild food. Have you ever seen a grown man pick at his food? I have, and I'd have to say that a little more physical labor might increase the appetite. There are a lot of soft handshakes out there. Occasionally I'll feel a rugged grip, somebody with some spring steel in their forearms, and it's generally a man of character. Honesty, decency, integrity, and reliability are great qualities to strive towards.

I'm a very independent person, and believe in doing everything for myself that I can. I believe it was Colonel Townsend Whelen that said "learn how to do everything." I do my own taxidermy work. Another good example might be that when I was ready to do the flooring in my house, I didn't hire someone to do it. I also didn't buy the materials to do it. I milled the wood from logs, and dried it myself. I didn't even buy the logs, and have them delivered to my saw mill. I cut the trees down on my property, and dragged them out myself. There's a great satisfaction in being self-sufficient, whether you're getting your own food, or working hard with your hands to create a thing of beauty that you can sit back and admire at the end of the day.

My woodshop is full of natures little secret treasures that come from the local woodlands. They have been hand-hewn, and their beauty exposed for all to see by myself, and others. There are chainsaw-carved bears, hand-carved Indians in drift wood, cedar boxes disguised as a cedar log until you pull the top off, birch log boxes, rustic furniture, tables with live edge and cedar log legs, cabinets that look like a half log that actually open, and all of it created with local wood, from the local woodlands.

Some of the prices on the bowls start at $15.00 so there is something for all price ranges. The floorboards of the woodshop are wide pine that I milled myself, the walls tongue and groove pine, and the outer walls log siding. That wooden box of a woodshop is near and dear to my heart. I look forward to going in every day, and smelling the mixture of fresh-cut pine and wood preservative, my tools laid out before me just waiting to create something.

My business — The North Country Whittler is located on Route 16 in Albany New Hampshire. It's just south of the town of Conway about eight miles in the White Mountains. I've been there for 12 years, and have owned it for eight, though I've been working with wood in some capacity since I was a teenager. My business has become somewhat of a landmark, and is easily noticed by the 40-foot tall Indian head in front of my shop. It's a real attention getter, and pulls plenty of traffic in off the road.

People are constantly asking me what my fascination is with the American Indian, and why I carve them. First off, there is a good deal of local history involving them, and many of the landmarks, towns and major roads in the area have Indian names. I carry no torch for the modern day Native American, and I also have no ill will toward them. My fascination is with the Indians of old, because they lived so close to the land. Everything they had from tools to food was provided by themselves directly from the land. They were self-sufficient, and free, though it was not an easy life. Live out of a tent for even a week, and then consider how many modern conveniences you have at your disposal, and you may get a slight idea of how hard their road must have been. They didn't live all too much differently than the wild animals. In some of the old black and white photos of the early American Indian you can see a wild look in there eyes.

Technology gadgets, and gizmos don't really thrill me all that much. I don't own a cell phone. There is something beautiful about simplicity. Kind of like the recurve bow. It doesn't have trigger releases and super duper arrow rests and gizmos all over like a compound bow. Stick and string — it's simple yet effective. It's smooth flowing lines and simplicity make it beautiful. People clutter there lives with too many trinkets that they really don't need. In a lot of instances, they are so far removed from God and nature that they try to fill the inner void with "things."

Satisfaction needs to come from within first, and then possessions add to the inner joy in our lives. The possessions themselves are not what create joy. In my way of thinking this is why happiness can prove so elusive to so many. It all starts in the outdoors, the answer to all of life's questions can be found there, yet in a modern world many never set foot in the woods. There has been an underlying current throughout this book that suggest there are many lessons to be learned from nature. You've heard me mention the outdoor classroom a few times. The American Indian of old was considered by many to be a savage, and furthermore, they never so much as attended elementary school. Why is it then that many of the Indian quotes, a few of which are located in this book, seem to contain such profound wisdom? Could it be that there truly is an education to be gained in the wilderness?

I'm often asked why I don't carry a cell phone when I hunt as I often hunt alone, and I usually mention something about not liking them much. Then the question comes up — well, what if something happens to you? I think people have gone overboard with safety. The safety police are everywhere. It goes back to being self-sufficient, self-reliant, and the satisfaction that comes from being that way. I can assure you I'm in no hurry to leave this world, I like it here just fine, but we're all going to leave sometime. Dick Proenneke said in his book, *One Man's Wilderness,* "when the time comes for a man to look his maker in the eye, where better could the meeting be held than in the wilderness."

I've been fortunate in that I seem to lead somewhat of a blessed and a charmed lifestyle. I've got a great family. I get to carve wood every day, and create things with my hands, and on top of that, people pay me to do it! I have a reasonable amount of time, and flexible schedule to pursue my hunting dreams. As my wife says "you've already lived quite the little hunting life." So, what about the author? I'd say family, work and the woods pretty much sum me up. Oh yeah, and I seldom forget to look up.

Index

Contact Information
for the Author and to Purchase Books

COLD SOULS
A Guide to Good Hunting
by Joshua W. Sargent is available through
your favorite book dealer or the publisher:

Whittler Woods Publishing
P.O. Box 105
West Ossipee, NH 03890
Telephone: 603-447-4921
Web site: www.coldsoulshuntingguide.com
E-mail: whittlerwoods@roadrunner.com

COLD SOULS
(ISBN: 978-0-9824849-0-6)
is $19.95 for softbound edition, plus $5.50 shipping
for first copy ($2.00 each additional copy).